D0939375

E
99
E7
M674
1997

CARIBOU HUNTERS
IN THE WESTERN ARCTIC

ZOOARCHAEOLOGY OF THE
RITA-CLAIRE AND BISON SKULL SITES

David A. Morrison

Mercury Series
Archaeological Survey of Canada
Paper 157

Published by
Canadian Museum of Civilization

APR 0 7 2003

© Canadian Museum of Civilization 1997

CANADIAN CATALOGUING IN PUBLICATION DATA

Morrison, David A.

Caribou hunters in the Western Arctic: zooarchaeology of the Rita-Claire and Bison Skull Sites

(Mercury series, ISSN 0316-1854)
(Paper/Archaeological Survey of Canada, ISSN 0317-2244; no. 157)
Includes bibliographical references.
Includes an abstract in French.
ISBN 0-660-15973-2

1   Inuvialuit Eskimos — Northwest Territories — Cape Bathurst — Antiquities.
2   Inuit — Territories — Cape Bathurst — Antiquities.
3   Rita-Claire Site (N.W.T.)
4   Bison Skull Site (N.W.T.)
5   Animal remains (Archaeology) — Northwest Territories — Cape Bathurst.
6   Cape Bathurst (N.W.T.) — Antiquities.
7   Excavations (Archaeology) — Northwest Territories — Cape Bathurst.
I   Canadian Museum of Civilization.
II   Title: Zooarchaeology of the Rita-Claire and Bison Skull Sites.
III Series.
IV Series: Paper (Archaeological Survey of Canada); no. 157.

E99.E7M67 1997   971.9'3'01   C97-980411-6

PRINTED IN CANADA

Published by
Canadian Museum of Civilization
100 Laurier Street
P.O. Box 3100, Station B
Hull, Quebec
J8X 4H2

Technical Editor: Richard Morlan
Coordination: Anne Malépart
Cover design: Roger Langlois Design

Front cover: Photos of caribou taken in the Arctic by David Morrison.

OBJECT OF THE MERCURY SERIES

The Mercury Series is designed to permit the rapid dissemination of information pertaining to the disciplines in which the Canadian Museum of Civilization is active. Considered an important reference by the scientific community, the Mercury Series comprises over three hundred specialized publications on Canada's history and prehistory.

Because of its specialized audience, the series consists largely of monographs published in the language of the author.

Titles in the Mercury Series can be obtained by calling in your order to 1-800-555-5621, or by writing to:

Mail Order Services
Canadian Museum of Civilization
100 Laurier Street
P.O. Box 3100, Station B
Hull, Quebec
J8X 4H2

BUT DE LA COLLECTION MERCURE

La collection Mercure vise à diffuser rapidement le résultat de travaux dans les disciplines qui relèvent des sphères d'activités du Musée canadien des civilisations. Considérée comme un apport important dans la communauté scientifique, la collection Mercure présente plus de trois cents publications spécialisées portant sur l'héritage canadien préhistorique et historique.

Comme la collection s'adresse à un public spécialisé, celle-ci est constituée essentiellement de monographies publiées dans la langue des auteurs.

Vous pouvez vous procurer la liste des titres parus dans la collection Mercure en appelant au 1 800 555-5621, ou en écrivant au :

Service des commandes postales
Musée canadien des civilisations
100, rue Laurier
C.P. 3100, succursale B
Hull (Québec)
J8X 4H2

Canada

Abstract

In 1992 and 1993, investigations were undertaken at two late precontact / early contact Inuvialuit (Inuit) archaeological sites in the western Canadian Arctic. The Rita-Claire and Bison Skull sites (OaRw-2 and -3) present a number of horizontally discrete activity areas relating to intensive caribou hunting, including an open-air habitation and processing area, a lookout and kill locality with shooting blinds, and a mass-slaughter bone bed. This study focuses on the analysis of the caribou remains from these three localities. Procedures for inferring the age and sex of caribou skeletons, and for analyzing patterns of bone fragmentation and destruction, are applied and assessed. Results suggest that the sites were occupied during the autumn, by people hunting caribou primarily through cooperative, communal techniques such as drives and ambushes. Density-mediated taphonomic factors such as organic decomposition and carnivore gnawing have left major, overwriting signatures in the faunal assemblages. But cultural activities such as marrow cracking can still be perceived, and important insights can be had into the economic activities and conditions of the people who occupied these sites 300 or 400 years ago.

Résumé

Des études sont entreprises, en 1992 et 1993, sur deux sites archéologiques inuvialuit (inuit) datant de la fin de la période du précontact et du début de celle du contact dans l'ouest de l'Arctique canadien. Les sites Rita-Claire et Bison Skull (OaRw-2 et OaRw-3) présentent un certain nombre d'aires d'activités, séparées les unes des autres horizontalement, en rapport avec une chasse au caribou intensive. On y trouve notamment une aire où on dressait des tentes et où s'effectuait le traitement des animaux, un lieu de guet et d'abattage avec des affûts et un dépôt important d'ossements résultant de la mise à mort d'un grand nombre de bêtes. Cette étude met l'accent sur l'analyse des restes de caribous de ces trois lieux. La procédure pour établir le sexe et l'âge des squelettes de caribous de même que pour analyser des modèles de fragmentation et d'élimination d'os est appliquée et évaluée. Les résultats laissent supposer que les sites étaient occupés à l'automne par des gens qui chassaient le caribou principalement de manière collective, coopérative, en utilisant des techniques telles que le rabattage et l'embuscade. Des facteurs taphonomiques liés à la densité de l'os tels que la décomposition organique et le rongement des carnivores ont marqué de façon importante les collections fauniques. Mais en dépit des actions naturelles, on peut encore voir des traces d'activités culturelles telles que l'écrasement des os pour en extraire la moelle, et on peut avoir un bon aperçu des activités et de la condition économiques des gens qui ont occupé ces sites il y a 300 ou 400 ans.

The Bison skull in 1987. A muskox skull is visible in the foreground.
Both have been flipped over from the original upside-down positions.

Foreward

Rita-Claire (OaRw-3) and Bison Skull (OaRw-2) are two closely adjacent archaeological sites located on the Old Horton River Channel, at the base of the Cape Bathurst Peninsula in the western part of the Canadian Arctic. Both were found in 1987 by Ray Le Blanc (n.d.), as part of the archaeology programme of the Canadian federal government's Northern Oil and Gas Action Plan (NOGAP). That summer I was excavating at the Iglulualuit site, on the other, eastern side of Cape Bathurst. One evening Le Blanc and Max Friesen, a field assistant, dropped in by helicopter and suggested I accompany them to visit some of the sites they had found. One in particular contained some partially-buried bone from some very large animal. They had found the site a few weeks earlier, when the ground surface was still frozen. Now, with the surface thawed, we were able to investigage a little more closely. The bone turned out to be the nearly complete skull of a bison, up-side-down in the ground, partially buried in the midst of what was evidently a relatively recent archaeological site. There were heavy cut marks on the frontal area, making its cultural association all the more obvious. Inevitably, we named the site Bison Skull.

We collected the skull and submitted it to Richard Harington of the Canadian Museum of Nature, who was very pleased to receive it. Bits of bison bone radiocarbon dated to about 5200 and 1800 years B.P. had been previously found at two locations in the Cape Bathurst area (Harington 1980, 1990). None of it, however, was complete enough to identify to species, and the later date, in particular, was considered suspiciously young. Could the western Arctic coast have supported a remnant bison population into late Holocene times? Our skull seems to confirm that the answer was "yes." It was complete enough that Harington was able to identify it as belonging to a smaller-than-average male wood bison (*Bison bison athabascae*, not *B. crassicornis* as reported by Le Blanc 1994: 7). Fresh bone from the specimen's interior yielded a uncalibrated, normalized radiocarbon date of 420 ± 65 years BP (Harington 1990; see chapter 2).

The OaRw-2 skull suggests that bison may have persisted in the area late enough to have been hunted by recent Inuvialuit (Inuit). It was to investigate this possibility that excavation was undertaken in 1992 and 1993, both at the Bison Skull site and at another nearby-by site we called Rita-Claire (OaRw-3). Not another scrap of bison bone, however, was found. Bison Skull and Rita-Claire are both Inuvialuit sites, and both date primarily to the late precontact period. But the overwhelming economic emphasis at both was on the hunting of caribou, not bison, and it is as caribou-hunting sites that they are presented here. The question of Inuvialuit bison hunting remains unresolved.

Acknowledgements

Work at the Rita-Claire and Bison Skull sites was funded by the Canadian Museum of Civilization's NOGAP Archaeology Project, with the generous assistance of the Polar Continental Shelf Project. I wish to thank my field crews — Claire Alix, Rita Elias, Verna Elias, Ben Felix, Gary Jessop, and James Mooney — for their hard work and dedication. The cooperation of the Inuvialuit Land Administration is acknowledged with thanks. Laboratory analysis was undertaken at the Canadian Museum of Civilization, with a few forays into the comparative collections at the Canadian Museum of Nature, for which Darlene Balkwill is to be thanked. The editorial assistance of Richard Morlan, and his help and advice with some of the more esoteric aspects of faunal analysis, is gratefully recorded here.

Table of Contents

List of Figures

Figure   Page

List of Tables

Chapter 1

Geographical and Cultural Setting

Cape Bathurst and the Old Horton Channel Area

The Rita-Claire and Bison Skull sites are located on the southern shore of the Old Horton River Channel, about 12 kilometres from its mouth at Harrowby Bay (Fig. 1.1, 1.2). The northern shore of the channel opposite the sites is relatively low-lying, sloping back gradually from the river as far as the eye can see. The southern shore, by contrast, consist of a narrow shaley beach below an abruptly-cut bluff face composed of unconsolidated sand, gravel and shale; a glaciofluvial deposit of Wisconsin age reaching a height of about 20 to 25 metres (Rampton 1988). From the top of this bluff stretches the flat and well-drained tableland of the Cape Bathurst Peninsula (Fig. 1.3), with the famous Smoking Hills just visible on the eastern horizon.

Every few hundred metres the shoreline bluffs are cut by short, small stream beds or gullies. They are an important feature of the local topography, acting as natural funnels for migrating caribou, who exhibit no great desire to climb the steep and treacherous bluff banks directly. Occasionally, too, these gullies cut back enough of the bank to produce small, grassy meadows at their mouths. Both the Rita-Claire and Bison Skull are located at stream mouths; Rita-Claire in particular taking advantage of one of the largest and flattest gully-meadows on the lower Channel. The streams which produce these gullies seem to flow only during the early summer melt, and are normally dry by early July.

At one time the Horton River flowed through the Old Horton Channel, meandering north and west past our two sites and into Harrowby Bay. About three or four hundred years ago, it broke through the Smoking Hills to flow east into Franklin Bay (Mackay 1981), leaving a semi-stagnant channel nearly a hundred kilometres long. This channel is archaeologically one of the richest areas in the western Canadian Arctic, with an inventory of several dozen sites (Le Blanc n.d.), including the important Crane site (Le Blanc 1994). Most date to the period before the Horton breakthrough, which must have been something of a local environmental disaster. No longer was fresh water flowing through the Channel in any volume, and with land subsidence the lower valley was drowned in sea water (the water at Rita-Claire and Bison Skull is brackish at best). Fish resources must have suffered dramatically, and driftwood was no longer carried down from the forested upper Horton valley. It is possible that the Rita-Claire and Bison Skull sites were occupied prior to the Horton breakthrough, and certain that they continued to be occupied after it. But as seasonal hunting camps the only clear effect the breakthrough would have

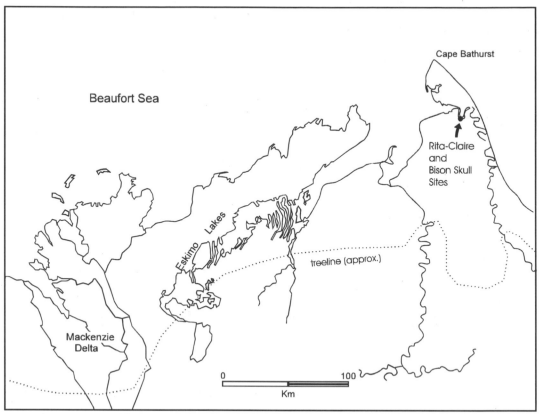

Figure 1.1. Location of the Rita-Claire and Bison Skull sites.

had would be to make drinking water more difficult to obtain.

Caribou are the most important wildlife resource in the area, and can be extremely numerous. Local animals are members of the Bluenose herd of barrenground caribou (*Rangifer tarandus groenlandicus*), which winter in the forests to the south and west, and calve along the Arctic coast from the Cape Bathurst Peninsula east to beyond Bluenose Lake (Martell et al. 1984: 41-42). Two other large herbivores are much rarer; moose (*Alces alces*), an occasional summer visitor from the south, and muskox (*Ovibos moschatus*). At present muskox are found no farther west than the upper Horton River valley, to the southeast of the study area, although in the 19th century they were fairly common as far west as the Anderson River (Martell et al. 1984: 61-62). Migratory waterfowl are abundant, and grizzly bears (*Ursus arctos*) can be seen on an almost daily basis during the summer. The seas support both ringed and bearded seal (*Phoca hispida* and *Erignathus barbatus*). Local vegetation is typical shrub tundra, dominated by species such as dwarf birch (*Betula nana*), willow (*Salix spp.*), Lapland rosebay (*Rhododendron lapponicum*), arctic heather (*Cassiope tetragona*) and various grasses.

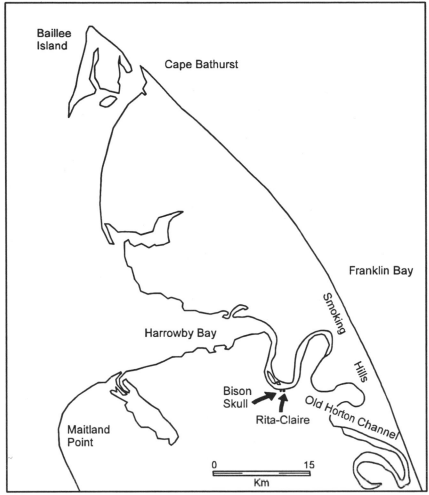

Figure 1.2. Map of Cape Bathurst.

The Traditional Economy of the Cape Bathurst Area

The Inuit inhabitants of the western Canadian Arctic refer to themselves as Inuvialuit, a name meaning "true human beings." At the time of European contact in the early 19th century, they were the richest and most populous group of Inuit in the Canadian Arctic, numbering approximately 2500 people. Like their Alaskan Inupiat neighbours to the west, they were divided into a number of politically and socially independent "nations." Most, at least, had a fairly well defined major village, for which they were named. Thus the Kittegaryumiut were "the people of Kittigazuit," the Nuvorugmiut were "the people of Nuvurak," the Gupugmiut were "the people of Gupuk," and so on. There were about six or seven such nations in the early 19th century, distributed from the northern Yukon coast to Franklin Bay (see Morrison 1990: Fig. 10). The precise number fluctuated over time — we know of one nation which disappeared in the immediate precontact period (Morrison and Arnold 1994) and another which vanished in the 1840s (Morrison 1990) — while in a few cases documentary evidence is not precise enough to allow clear identifications.

The Rita-Claire and Bison Skull sites are located within the traditional territory of the second most easterly of these nations; the Avvagmiut, named for their chief village of Avvaq on one of the Baillie Islands just off-shore from Cape Bathurst (see Stefansson 1914: 25ff; Usher 1971; McGhee 1974). Documentary sources suggest that most Avvagmiut spent the late summer, open-water season hunting bowhead whales from Avvaq and a nearby village at Cape Bathurst itself, apparently named Utkalluk (Stefansson 1914: 25; Richardson 1851: 266-268; M'Clure 1969: 93; Pullen 1979: 114-120).

During August, the total population of these two villages was probably on the order of about 500 people. In autumn they dispersed to fish and hunt caribou in the interior. In early winter people moved into their sod-and-driftwood winter houses, mostly in the Avvaq-Cape Bathurst area, although Pullen (1979: 113-114) mentions another winter-house village at Maitland Point . During this season people lived mainly off food stored from the summer-autumn period. Seals were also taken with nets set under the ice (Stefansson 1914: 350). With the return of the sun, and as winter supplies ran out, people moved out onto the sea ice where they lived in snowhouse villages and hunted ringed seals at their breathing holes, much like their eastern neighbours in the Central Arctic (see Jenness 1922). Finally, when the sea ice began to melt in the spring people moved inland again, where they fished and hunted until the bowhead season began in early August.

Caribou were hunted throughout most of the warmer seasons of the year. Even during the August whale hunt, it is likely that not everyone abandoned the interior, for August and early September hides were preferred for skin clothing (Stefansson 1914: 149). By late September hides were becoming too thick for most clothing purposes and the focus began to shift to more intensive meat hunting, since during this season caribou (particularly the bulls) are at their nutritional best, and conditions are cold enough that meat can be stored without a great deal of effort. By contrast, the spring/early summer hunt may have been a much more casual, hand-to-mouth affair. Spring and early summer caribou hides are worthless for clothing and the animals themselves are so lean that most Inuit considered them to be hardly worth eating, except as an occasional change of diet (see Jenness 1922: 123; Burch 1991). MacFarlane (1905: 681), for instance, records that the Anderson River Inuvialuit hunted caribou during the spring, "on their annual migration to the coast," but "especially on their fall return to the woods," and it is likely their Cape Bathurst kinsmen did the same. Waterfowl and fish were probably more important during the spring and early summer.

Bowhead whales, of course, can also supply a very large food surplus. One mid-19th century visitor described how after a successful season the whale hunters at Cape Bathurst spent early winter "revel(ling) in greasy abundance" (Richardson 1851: 348). However, like other Inuvialuit the Avvagmiut were less successful bowhead hunters than their north Alaskan kinsmen. Only two or three whales were taken in an average year, and sometimes none at all (Richardson 1851: 267), probably because whales do not enter the eastern Beaufort Sea - Amundsen Gulf area until the open water season (Fraker and Bockstoce 1980), when hunting them is far

Figure 1.3. The Cape Bathurst Peninsula. Much of it is a well-drained, rolling plateau,
providing excellent pasture for caribou.

more difficult than under the spring, ice-lead conditions of the Alaskan hunt (see Rainey 1947).

Probably not all Avvagmiut had equal access to the bowhead hunt and its proceeds. Like other Inuvialuit, the Avvagmiut were an incipiently ranked society (Morrison 1988, in press), and wealth — particularly wealth resulting from such a high-status occupation as whaling — tended to be concentrated in the hands of a few well-connected, powerful individuals (*"umialit"*) and their immediate families and supporters. Some idea of the relationship between coastal whalers and interior caribou-hunters can be gleaned from a traditional Inuvialuit story called "The Whale Hunt" (Schwarz 1970: 46-54). It describes a shamanic duel between two *umialit* who lived on the Tuktoyaktuk Peninsula. The loser was unable to hunt whales anymore. "Eventually,

quite impoverished," the story concludes, "he had to abandon the sea and move south where he became a caribou hunter." Especially for some, the caribou hunt was of crucial importance.

The Rita-Claire and Bison Skull sites provide a rare archaeological window on this important aspect of the local economy. They are the only Inuvialuit archaeological sites from the interior of the Cape Bathurst Peninsula to have ever been excavated, and among only a handful of productive Inuit sites from anywhere in the Arctic which relate entirely to the open-air, warm weather seasons of the year, when people lived in tents rather than winter houses. Unfortunately, their large coastal counterparts at Cape Bathurst, Bailee Island, and Maitland Point have been almost totally destroyed by land subsidence.

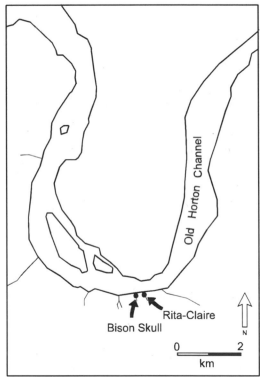

Figure 2.1. Setting of the Rita-Claire and Bison Skull sites, Old Horton Channel.

The Bison Skull site (OaRw-2)

The Bison Skull site is located around the mouth of a substantial stream gully on the southern shore of the Old Horton Channel (Fig. 2.1). The site is well located for the interception of caribou migrating across the channel, which seems to have been its main function. The higher slopes command an excellent view, particularly to the north, where the great loop of the channel acts like a magnet drawing migrating caribou south. Deep drifts of caribou hair along the high-water mark indicate that it is still commonly used as a crossing spot (Fig. 2.2).

Essentially the site can be divided into two relatively discrete areas, Bison Skull East and Bison Skull West (Fig. 2.3).

Bison Skull West

The western component of the Bison Skull site consists of a very dense concentration of buried and partially buried bone, almost all of it assignable to caribou. It covers an area of at least 10 x 20 metres on the grassy western slope of the gully, about forty metres from the water and about eight metres above it. Because of the steepness of this slope, about 25 degrees, there is a clear tendency for bone to erode out of the bank and roll down it embedded within clumps of sod (see Fig. 2.4). Worked caribou metapodial fragments (see Morrison 1986) were commonly observed, and several crania were noted with the antlers hacked and sawed off. Judging by the extent and denseness of the concentration, this western portion of the site must represent the skeletal remains of no fewer than several hundred caribou, and possibly many more.

Figure 2.2. Drifts of caribou hair along the beach at the Bison Skull site.

A single 1 x 1 m test pit was excavated just east of the visible surface bone, in a flatter area with a more stable, grassy surface. It produced an immense quantity of caribou bone from just below the sod to a depth of 30 to 35 cm, in so dense a concentration that there was far more bone than soil. This excavated bone was collected and will be described in detail below. Artifactial material included cut antler (including at least two sawed pieces) and three pieces of metapodial debitage. The test pit also yielded a broken antler fishhook shank of typical Inuvialuit form, a stone net sinker, and four cortical, lithic flakes (two of quartizite and two of chert). The sparse matrix was an undifferentiated gravelly sand.

The main function of Bison Skull West bone bed seems fairly clear; it is a primary caribou butchering area, and one of fairly major portions. However, the presence of a few pieces of non-caribou bone and the fishing shank and sinker suggest that more than just the butchering (and possibly the killing) of caribou took place here. Unfortunately, a more complete investigation of Bison Skull West was not possible because of time constraints.

A caribou bone sample from the test pit was submitted for radiocarbon analysis, and yielded a normalized, uncalibrated date of 70 ± 50 B.P. (Beta-94895) (Table 2.1). According to the Beta laboratory report, the calibrated results at the 2-sigma or 95% probability range indicate a calendar date either between A.D. 1680 and 1755, or between A.D. 1805 and 1940, with no intercept of the radiocarbon age with the calibration curve.

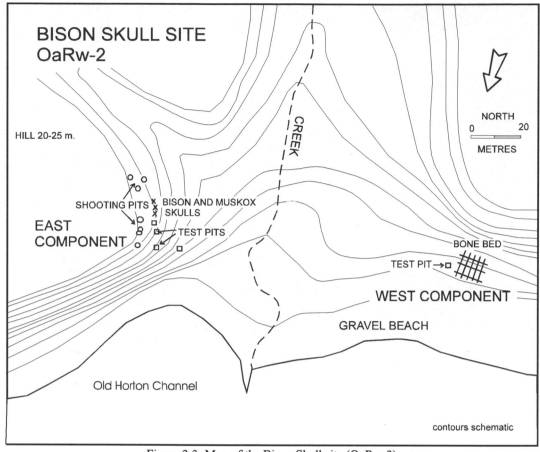

Figure 2.3. Map of the Bison Skull site (OaRw-2).

This is a considerable period of time, and one which can be narrowed down with reference to the recovered material only with difficulty. The lithic flakes, the absence of European trade goods (although the sample is very small), and perhaps the traditional fishhook shank all seem to preclude a 20th century date. On the other hand, the sawing of bone and antler may imply the use of metal saws, which would have been unavailable in the area before about 1800 (see Morrison 1988: 1-11, 1991). The large size of the bone bed might even suggest a commercially-motivated hunt aimed at provisioning American whaling ships during the whaling era

in the western Arctic (ca. 1890-1910), when ships over-wintered as nearby as Cape Bathurst (see Bockstoce 1986). Overall, a 19th century date is probably the best estimate for the site's occupation.

Bison Skull East

The eastern component of the Bison Skull site is located at and just below the top of the gully hill to the east of the site creek (Fig. 2.5, 2.6). It was here on a narrow break in the slope that the bison skull was found, flanked by two partially buried muskox skulls. Above the skulls and just below the edge of the hill

Figure 2.4. Sod blocks containing embedded caribou bone roll down the hill at Bison Skull West.

Figure 2.5. The hill at Bison Skull East.

Figure 2.7. Shooting blind at the top of the hill at Bison Skull East.

Figure 2.8. Hide pegs from Bison Skull East.

top are seven shooting pits arranged in a rough line. Each is about 1.2 metres in diameter - large enough to have concealed a single hunter - and dug perhaps 30 cm into the soft ground surface, in an area of low shrub willows (Fig. 2.7). Excavation in three of the pits produced small quantities of broken caribou and bird bone (the latter possibly representing a fox kill), and two wooden hide pegs.

More hide pegs were found on the top of the hill. Here the ground is very flat, and supports only the sparsest vegetation. Several dozen wooden pegs were spread out on the ground surface over an area of about 15 x 15 metres. They averaged 15 to 20 cm in length and were roughly sharpened at one end (Fig.2.8).

Four 1 x 1 metre test pits were excavated in the general area of the bison skull. All produced fairly abundant broken caribou and other bone from immediately below the modern sod to an average depth of about 20 cm, in an undifferentiated matrix of sand and gravel. Along with the bone was a fairly considerable range of artifacts, including three more hide pegs, a caribou-scapula sidescraper or "fish scaler," a bowdrill mouth-piece made on a caribou astragalus (Fig. 2.9), a typical Inuvialuit sinew twister (for tightening the sinew backing on a bow) (Fig. 2.10,a), an antler arrowhead (Fig. 2.10,b), two bone awls, a slate endblade, a slate ulu blade fragment, several broken antler wedges, three caribou metapodial blanks, 11 antler flakes produced by adzing, 25 other pieces of bone or antler debitage, six unidentified antler tool fragments, five typical Inuvialuit pottery sherds (total weight 40 grams), 69 chert flakes and shatter fragments (total weight of 130.3 grams), 111 quartzite flakes (418 grams), two sandstone or granite flakes (11 grams), 17 siliceous shale flakes (20.8 grams), and a single tiny flake of fused shale or clinker (0.3 grams). This clinker is a heat-altered material produced in the smouldering bocannes of the Smoking Hills, abundantly attested in local Palaeoeskimo assemblages (see Le Blanc 1994: 52ff), but generally rare in Neoeskimo contexts. The other lithic materials are widely available in local tills.

Bison Skull East obviously served a number of purposes, not all of them, perhaps, at the same time. It commands a fine view, and doubtless served as a look-out. The shooting pits indicate that caribou were killed in the immediate area, presumably with bows and arrows, and quite probably as part of an organized drive or drives (see Jenness 1922: 148-151 for a description of how such drives might have worked). Other activities seem to include the staking of hides and possibly the butchering of carcasses, along with tool manufacture and repair. No hearths, tent rings,

Table 2.1. Radiocarbon dates for the Rita-Claire and Bison Skull sites.

Site	Material	Lab. No.	Uncorrected Age rcybp	Normalized Age rcybp*	Calibration (A.D.)**
Bison Skull East	caribou bone	Beta-94895	modern	70±50	1680 1700-1720 1755 1805 1820-1855 1860-1920 1940
Bison Skull West	caribou bone	Beta-94896	190±50	280±50	1485 1525-1560 1630 [1650] 1665 1675 1770-1800 1940-1950
Bison Skull West	bison bone	Beta-28765	not available	420±65	1410 1430 [1455] 1610 1590-1620 1645
Rita-Claire	caribou bone	Beta-94897	200±100	300±100	1425 1470 [1640] 1670 1780-1795 1890 1905 1945-1950 1950
Rita-Claire	caribou bone	Beta-94898	220±70	320±70	1440 1475 [1535 1545 1635] 1655 1675 1770-1800 1940-1950
Rita-Claire	caribou bone	S-3549	modern	-	-

* normalization based on estimated $^{13}C/^{12}C$ ratio of -19.0 ‰; ** underlined values are 2-sigma limits, intercepts shown in square brackets.

or other indications of a habitation area were observed.

One of the test squares was situated within half a metre of where the bison skull was found. A caribou-bone sample excavated from a depth of 15 cm from this square was submitted for radiocarbon analysis. It yielded an uncalibrated, normalized date of 280±50 B.P. (Beta-94896) (see Table 2.1), with three calibrated date ranges at the 2-sigma level: A.D. 1485 to 1675, A.D. 1770 to 1800, and A.D. 1940 to 1950. At the 1-sigma level there are only two calibrated date ranges: A.D. 1525 to 1560 and A.D. 1630 to 1665. The intercept of the radiocarbon age with the calibration curve is A.D. 1650. Of the three 2-sigma ranges the last — A.D. 1940-1950 — is clearly precluded by the absence from this site area of any evidence of European contact, including sawed bone and antler. Bison Skull East can thus be dated at a 95% confidence level to the period A.D. 1485 to 1800, and at a 68% confidence level to the period A.D. 1525 to 1665. Nothing in the artifact assemblage contradicts this conclusion.

It is possible but perhaps unlikely that the eastern and western components of the Bison Skull site are contemporaneous. The radiocarbon dates overlap at the 2-sigma level, but artifactual evidence suggest that Bison Skull East is largely or entirely pre-contact, while Bison Skull West may date to the post-contact period.

It is interesting to compare the Bison Skull East date with that obtained on the bison skull itself (Beta-28765), submitted by Richard Harington (1990; see Table 2.1 for additional information not published by Harington). The uncalibrated, normalized date is 420±65 BP, with one calibrated date range at the 2-sigma level — A.D. 1410 to 1645 — and two ranges at the 1-sigma level: A.D. 1430-1510 and

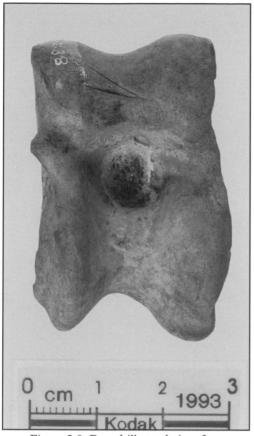

Figure 2.9. Bow drill mouthpiece from
Bison Skull East.

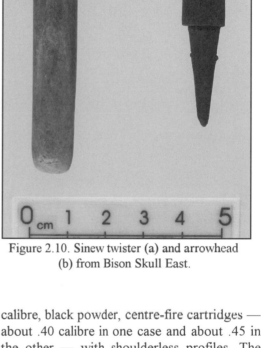

Figure 2.10. Sinew twister (a) and arrowhead
(b) from Bison Skull East.

A.D. 1590-1620. The date on the skull and that on caribou bone in the skull area thus overlap even at the 1-sigma level. The skull must be considered at least generally contemporaneous with the occupation area in which it was found.

Isolated Finds

The beach in front of the Bison Skull site produced a few isolated finds. One is a native copper bracelet, similar to specimens from the Coronation Gulf area (Morrison 1983: Pl. 26, a-b), from where it was probably traded. Also found were two brass cartridge cases. The head stamps are illegible, but both are large

calibre, black powder, centre-fire cartridges — about .40 calibre in one case and about .45 in the other — with shoulderless profiles. The smaller calibre example seems to be a .38-55 Winchester and Ballard, introduced in 1884 (Barnes 1980: 75) and a very popular cartridge locally during the late 19th and early 20th centuries (Stefansson 1914: 273).

The Rita-Claire Site (OaRw-3)

The Rita-Claire site is located on the next gully mouth upstream from Bison Skull, a distance along the beach of about 150 metres. It occupies a beautiful grassy meadow at the mouth of the gully, about a metre-and-a-half

Figure 2.11. Bone eroding out at the beach cut at Rita-Claire.

above the level of the Old Horton Channel. The site is plainly marked by a layer of bone eroding out from beneath the sod cap of the meadow at the top of the beach line (Fig. 2.11). Informal shovel testing and four formal 1 x 1 metre test pits, however, indicate that the occupation is a very discontinuous one, mostly concentrated in the area of the excavation block (Fig. 2.12). An unknown but probably significant portion of the site has been lost to erosion.

One very curious feature of the site is a line of 53 caribou skulls on the hill leading up from the site meadow from the south (Fig. 2.13-2.14). They are badly weathered, without mandibles or usually much of the rostrum, and are arranged over a distance of about 60 metres. Most are well sunk into the sod, while others perch on the surface. The line they define is a relatively straight one, despite their position on a very steep hill (at least 30 degrees), which would tend to encourage rolling. The meaning of this feature is obscure, but keeping in mind the bison and two muskox skulls at the Bison Skull site we may suspect some spiritual or religious significance. Interior North Alaskan Inuit (Inupiat) performed post-hunt rituals which focussed on the severed heads of caribou, aimed at propitiating their spirits and ensuring their re-birth (Spencer 1959: 356-7). How the heads were disposed of in this ritual is unclear, nor has anything similar been recorded of the Inuvialuit, although considering the poor ethnographic record from the area this is not

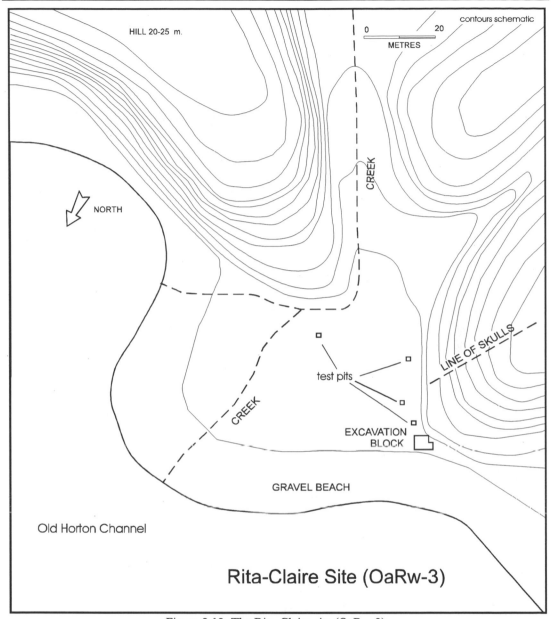

Figure 2.12. The Rita-Claire site (OaRw-3).

surprising. The line of caribou skulls at Rita-Claire may witness some kind of ritual which similarly focussed on severed caribou heads.

An area encompassing 18 square metres was excavated on the meadow bottom. Cultural material was found from immediately beneath the thin, modern sod to 50 cm depth, when excavation was brought to a halt by the end of the final field season. The great majority of the cultural material, however, came from between about 10 and 35 cm depth; after 40 cm very little was recovered beyond the occasional flake and animal bone

Figure 2.13. Line of caribou skulls at the Rita-Claire site.

Figure 2.14. Surficial caribou skulls, from the "line of skulls," at the Rita-Claire site.

fragment. It seems likely that there has been considerable vertical displacement due to frost action and/or mechanical processes like trampling. Unfortunately, beyond a weakly developed humic layer the site displayed no clear horizontal stratigraphy. The soil matrix was a fine, medium-brown soil very heavily mixed with shale, interlensed with a few thin patches of peaty, organic material. The proportion of shale gradually increased with increased depth, and the matrix as a whole is probably of colluvial origin. It was damp but relatively well-drained, and permafrost was rarely encountered. Organic preservation, perhaps because of the acidic nature of the shale, tended to be poor by arctic standards, and animal bones were sometimes found in a soft, degraded state, with a consistency like wet cardboard.

Because of the absence of stratigraphy, excavation proceeded in 10 cm horizontal levels. Floor plans were kept for each level, recording the positions of artifacts and features (Fig. 2.15-2.17), and faunal material was collected by level for each excavation unit. Because of time constraints and the very shaley nature of the deposit, only bone and lithic flake concentrations were screened.

Five small but well-defined hearths were the most prominent features encountered. One had a top 11 cm below ground surface (Fig. 2.15), and four others, all of them closely adjacent, had tops between 21 and 26 cm below surface (Fig. 2.16). One of the latter was triple lobed and may actually represent three different but overlapping hearths. With tops at different heights none otherwise

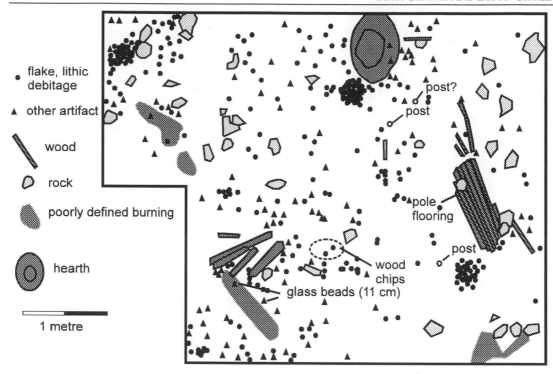

Figure 2.15. Rita-Claire planview, 10-20 cm depth.

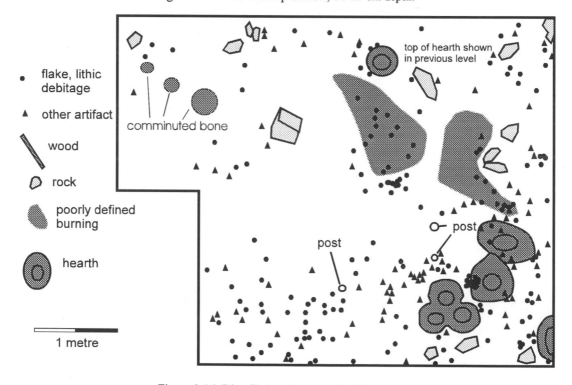

Figure 2.16. Rita-Claire planview, 20-30 cm depth.

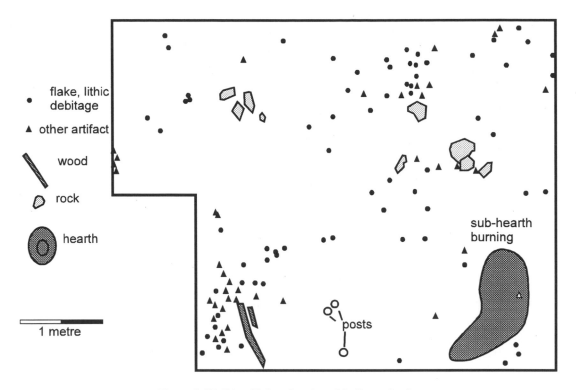

Figure 2.17. Rita-Claire planview, 30-40 cm depth.

appears exactly contemporaneous with another, and none could be associated with a clear occupation floor. All share a similar bowl-shaped profile, 8 to 12 cm thick, with ash and fire-reddened earth but no hearth stones. Near the topmost hearth (at 11 cm) lay a group of narrow poles, each over a metre long and about 2 cm wide, placed side-by-side, and suggesting part of the floor of some very light structure, presumably a tent. Poorly defined burned areas encountered at different depths may represent more short-term hearths or informal fires.

No clear evidence of any kind of occupation structure was found, beyond the small area of possible flooring already described. Most or all of the rocks in the deposit matrix seem to be naturally occurring, and there is no indication of a patterned arrangement which might be interpreted as a

tent ring. A few wooden posts or stakes were encountered, broken off short in the ground, but again forming no apparent pattern, while the general distribution of artifacts does not suggest any distinction between an "inside" and an "outside." Given the arctic climate, the season of occupation (see below), and the clear absence of a heavy "winter" sod house, it seems very likely that the site's inhabitants did live in tents. Either they were placed outside the excavation area or they left no recognizable remains.

Artifacts

Excavations at Rita-Claire yielded 2108 artifacts. By far the most common were items associated with lithic reduction, including five relatively formalized flake cores (three of quartzite weighing 420.4 grams, two of chert weighing 246.5 grams), and 1583 lithic flakes

Figure 2.18. Nuwuk harpoon head *in situ* at the Rita-Claire site (length = 4.4 cm).

Table 2.2. Lithic flakes and shatter fragments: Rita-Claire site.

material	n	grams
chert	815	1687.9
quartzite	653	2226.5
fused clinker	60	55.3
siliceous argillite	54	34.2
Thunder River shale	1	0.4

and shatter fragments (see Table 2.2). Lithic materials include local cherts, quartzites and siliceous argillites, fused clinker from the Smoking Hills, and one tiny, exotic flake of Thunder River fused shale (Pilon 1990).

Pottery sherds were also abundant; 29 rim sherds and 230 body sherds, all of the coarse plain-ware common to western Arctic Inuit sites. Two distinct vessel forms are well represented. One is beaker shaped, with straight, cylindrical sides, a flat base, and a straight lip. One partially-complete vessel stands 72 mm high and has a diameter of 77.2 mm. The second vessel shape is more rounded or globular in outline, with a rounded, markedly thickened lip, pierced in a nearly vertical direction by narrow punctates formed when the clay was still wet. The punctates may be decorative, and possibly they helped dry the clay prior to firing; their tiny diameter (ca. 2.5 mm) and position near the rim seeems

to preclude their use as suspension holes. The fabric of this punctated vessel or vessels is noticeably softer and more friable than that used in the beaker-shaped vessels.

Debitage from the manufacture of tools from bone and antler is represented. There are 59 pieces of cut or hacked debitage (including 20 antler chips or flakes produced with an adze), 17 bone and antler tool blanks, and 17 cut antler tines. As at Bison Skull, the antler was typical light and spongey in texture, suggesting that it was in velvet when deposited in the site.

Most categories of functionally identifiable tools are represented by only a few specimens. Included are nine chipped-stone triangular and tear-drop shaped arrow points or endblades (five of chert and four of fused clinker), three bone and antler arrowheads (one with a gouged endblade slot), a bow shim, a small Nuwuk harpoon head (Fig. 2.18) and two fragmentary harpoon endblades - one slate (Fig. 2.19, a) and the other bone - a light harpoon socketpiece made of whale bone (Fig. 2.19, b), two antler or whale bone snow probes (Fig. 2.19, c-d), three bird-dart prongs, a fishnet float and gauge (Fig. 2.20), a bone fish hook, an ivory composite knife handle, two graver handles, a ground-stone adze blade, a bone marrow spoon, four caribou-scapula sidescrapers ("fish-scalers"), eight slate ulu blades, some of them fragmentary, 16 marginally utilized or retouched flakes (nine clinker, six chert, one quartzite), five chipped-stone endscrapers (one clinker and four quartzite) with a long antler endscraper handle, a bone sewing needle, and a top-hat shaped limestone labret. The collection also includes 13 mostly fragmentary "fine bifaces" neatly chipped from chert or fused clinker (Fig. 2.21). Most appear to have functioned as knives or weapon tips.

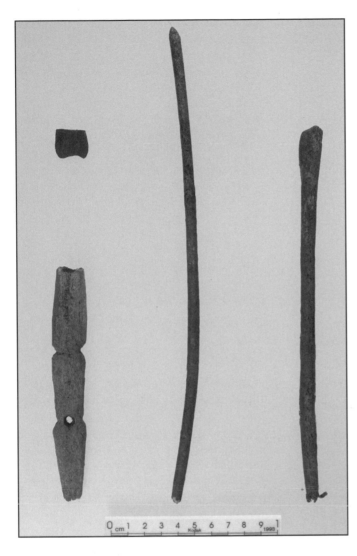

Figure 2.19. Hunting and travelling gear, Rita-Claire site.

summer/autumn nature of the occupation, when work could be accomplished out-of-doors and raw materials were easily available in local tills. Chipped stone debitage, for instance, was also very abundant at Gutchiak (Morrison 1994), another open-air, warm-weather Inuvialuit site, but is much rarer in winter house sites (e.g. Morrison 1990). Pottery was clearly used and broken in considerable quantities. Also very well attested is evidence of large-animal butchering and hide processing, comprising numerous end scrapers, biface knives, ulus, a scraper handle, and a broken sewing needle. Terrestrial hunting gear is likewise fairly abundant, including bird-dart prongs and both bone and lithic arrow tips. Less well represented are sea mammal gear (harpoon head and endblades, socketpiece) and especially the fishing gear (net gauge, net float, fish hook) so common on most other Inuvialuit sites (eg. McGhee 1974; Morrison 1994; Swayze 1994).

Like all Inuit, the Inuvialuit had a highly structured, "curated" (Binford 1979) tool kit, and it would be foolish to expect too direct a correlation between the immediate subsistence function of a site and its excavated tool assemblage. Yet on a general level, the relative proportions of these functionally related items sees some reflection in the faunal remains, which indicate an almost exclusive focus on the hunting, butchering, and processing of caribou. The possibility that many or most of these caribou were killed at

It has been clear for some time that there is little temporal or geographic variation in precontact Inuvialuit tool assemblages (McGhee 1974), and the artifacts from Rita-Claire (and for that matter Bison Skull) compare well with those from most other recent western Arctic sites. The abundance of chipped lithic debris is striking, and may be in part a function of the open-air,

Figure 2.20. Bone net gauge, Rita-Claire site.

the nearby Bison Skull site is something to keep in mind as we examine the faunal assemblage.

Dating

Two radiocarbon samples were submitted to the Beta lab from the Rita-Claire site, both caribou bone (Table 2.1). One (Beta-94897) came from the same level (20-30 cm) as the four lower hearths, and yielded a normalized radiocarbon date of 300 ± 100 radiocarbon years B.P. Calibrated results at the two-signa level suggest two date ranges: A.D. 1425 to 1890, and A.D. 1905 to 1950. At the one-sigma level there are three age ranges indicated: A.D. 1470 to 1670, A.D. 1780 to 1795, and A.D. 1945 to 1950.

The second sample (Beta-94898) came from the same unit, but near the bottom of the site (30 to 40 cm). It yielded a normalized date of 320 ± 70 B.P., with three calibrated results at the two-sigma level: A.D. 1440-1675, A.D. 1770-1800, and A.D. 1940-1950. At the one-sigma level one a single calibrated range is indicated: A.D. 1475 to 1655. It can be noted that the two dates are in stratigraphic order, but are not greatly dissimilar.

Small quantities of historic trade material were found at Rita-Claire; two blue glass beads and three small fragments of iron (one a vessel fragment). All three iron fragments came from within the upper 10 cm of the site, while both blue beads (they were found about 40 cm apart) came from a depth of 11-12 cm, about the same depth but several metres away from the uppermost hearth. Also recovered from the uppermost 10 cm were five small pieces of sawed antler. These few items suggest a terminal occupation date for the site in the 19th or even very late in the 18th century, when such trade goods were first entering the western Canadian Arctic (see Morrison 1991). By extension, the lower, radiocarbon-dated units of the site, which did not produce trade goods, were occupied before this. By excluding the post-A.D. 1800 portions of the calibrated radiocarbon ages, it can be suggested that the site was initially occupied sometime between about A.D. 1425 and 1670, but no date in the last few hundred years before contact is precluded. The similarity between the two dates for Rita-

Figure 2.21. Fine bifaces, Rita-Claire site.

Claire and the single radiocarbon date for Bison Skull East is striking. Rita-Claire may (or may not) have been occupied over a longer span, but within the limits of radiocarbon dating the two sites may be considered contemporaneous.

A third radiocarbon sample from Rita-Claire was submitted to the Saskatchewan rather than the Beta lab (S-3549). It produced a measured ^{14}C age of less than 100 years, with no attempt to correct for fractionation. Coming from the very bottom of the excavation, at nearly 50 cm, this third date seems to contribute nothing useful to a discussion of the age of the site.

Chapter 3

The Faunal Assemblages

A considerable amount of faunal material was recovered from the relatively modest excavations undertaken at the Bison Skull and Rita-Claire sites. This chapter briefly presents an overview of the three assemblages, analytical methods and assumptions, and an investigation of seasonality.

Methods and Assumptions

All faunal analysis involves various degrees of uncertainty, and is based upon assumptions and methods which are too often unstated (Driver 1992). Some of the basic or conditioning assumptions and methods used in this study are described here.

Aggregation Units

As Grayson (1984) in particular has argued, the aggregation units used in any faunal analysis will have a profound effect upon results. Unfortunately the nature of the site data provides little choice in the matter at Rita-Claire and Bison Skull. The Bison Skull site is separated into two horizontally discrete components, but it is not possible to subdivide either site vertically. At Rita-Claire, especially, it appears that the site was occupied over a significant period of time. However, without clear internal stratigraphy it is impossible to define exclusive aggregation units within the overall site framework. A comparison of material from each of the 10-cm arbitrary excavation levels suggests no obvious differences in faunal frequencies from top to bottom, but no doubt there was a considerable range of more subtle variation which is beyond investigation. All three components, then, are presented as unitary entities, despite the fact that Rita-Claire

certainly, Bison Skull East probably, and Bison Skull West possibly, do not represent single occupational or use events.

Identification

All faunal identifications were made by comparisons with documented reference specimens, beginning with those in the zooarchaeological collection of the Canadian Museum of Civilization. This collection has its gaps and weaknesses which impose various limitations to analysis. This was particularly the case with regard to birds and fishes, identified under contract by Leslie Still (1996a, 1996b, 1996c). In most cases no attempt was made to identify specimens in these classes to species, because they could not be directly supported by the comparative collection. Most identifications were made to some higher taxon, such as cod (Family Gadidae) or geese (Tribe Anserini). No attempt was made to pursue identification beyond this level because of time, expense, and the major focus of the study, which is the mammalian fauna, particularly the caribou.

The mammalian fauna, identified by the author, was considered in more detail. Here every attempt was made to identify to the species level, and in cases where the Canadian Museum of Civilization collection was inadequate recourse was had to the much more complete collections of the Canadian Museum of Nature.

Lyman (1994a: 100) suggests that "it is typically necessary to identify the skeletal element prior to identifying the taxon represented by a specimen," and above the Class level this is almost invariably true.

Table 3.1. Mammalian body size categories.

Size	Weight	Examples
1	<100 g	mice, voles, lemmings, ermine
2	100-700 g	groundsquirrel
3	700-5000 g	red and arctic fox, marten, muskrat, hares
4	5-25 kg	small dog, wolverine, juvenile caribou, (lynx)
5	25-200 kg	caribou, wolf, large dog
6	200+ kg	grizzly or polar bear, moose, muskox, (bison)

However, many specimens which could not be identified to element were assignable to Class (mammal, bird, fish) on the basis of size, shape, and texture. Indeed most specimens which could only be identified to the Class level could not be identified to specific element. Many specimens, particularly rib and longbone fragments, which were too fragmentary to be identified taxonomically above the Class level were still sufficiently complete to be sorted into body-size categories (Table 3.1). Ideally, this procedure could be employed with birds or even fishes, but for this study it was restricted to mammals. The body-size categories employed have been adapted from Dyck and Morlan (1995) and Thomas (1969).

Identification to higher taxa is based on assumptions about what species could be present; otherwise the task becomes either impossible or pointlessly pedantic (Driver 1992: 44). For a recent archaeological site located in so ecologically simple an environment as the Arctic, the list of available species is a relatively short one and the task relatively easy, although the presence of a bison skull warns against too narrow an approach. Essentially it is assumed that the modern fauna and the fauna of three or four hundred years ago are similar, and that animals had ranges and behavioral patterns similar to today. Thus a mandible fragment which can be identified only as belonging to a medium-sized artiodactyl on its own strict merits is classified specifically as "caribou," even though it lacks diagnostic portions which would clearly distinguish it from white-tailed deer, for instance, or saiga antelope. In a different kind of environment, or at a greater time depth, this assumption would not be warranted. We are not, it is hoped, falling guilty of what Driver

(1992: 44) refers to as "identification by association," for it is the local biosphere which is assumed to be relatively stable (at least over the past few hundred years), not the composition of an assemblage. The list of local mammals presented in Table 3.1 is essentially complete for mammals larger than size category 1 (i.e. greater than 100 grams in weight), except that it does not include sea mammals.

Quantification

Faunal analysis is a discipline beset by numbers and systems of quantification (Ringrose 1993, Lyman 1994b). Chief among these are the NISP ("number of identified specimens"), MNI ("minimum number of individuals"), and MAU ("minimum animal units"). All have their uses and their limitations and have been widely discussed in the literature (e.g. Grayson 1984, Ringrose 1993, Lyman 1994b). In this study and elsewhere, MNI and NISP are chiefly useful for comparing frequencies between taxa, while the MAU (Binford 1981, 1984) is used for comparing anatomical-part frequencies within a taxon. Following standard usage, the calculation of MNIs considers side, size, and state of epiphyseal fusion, while the calculation of MAUs does not. MNIs per skeletal portion (Lyman 1994a: 103) can never be less than the corresponding MAU, and are almost invariably greater.

Less has been written on the MNE or "minimum number of elements," and it is here that major problems of comparability exist. The MNE, although basic to the calculation of other statistics, is itself rarely presented in published reports, much less discussed. Different ways of calculating the MNE can

Table 3.2. Features used in counting minimum number of elements.

Element	Counting Feature
Cranium	Frontlet, auditory bullae, maxillary foramen, posterior maxillary alveolus, M3, anterior maxillary alveolus, P2
Mandible	Articular condyle, posterior alveolus, m3, anterior alveolus, p2, mental foramen
Atlas	Posterior zygapophyses
Axis	Centrum, neural spine (at neural canal)
Cervical vertebrae	Centrum, neural spine (at neural canal)
Thoracic vertebrae	Centrum, neural spine (at neural canal)
Lumbar vertebrae	Centrum, neural spine (at neural canal)
Sacrum	Anterior epiphysis
Innominate	Acetabulum, ilium (tuber sacrale, acetabulum), ischium ("rolled" ischial border, acetabulum), pubis (acetabulum)
Rib	Head (articular facet)
Scapula	Distal articular end, nutrient foramen
Humerus, proximal	Lateral tuberosity (articular end), teres tuberosity (shaft)
Humerus, distal	Coronoid fossa (articular end), posterolateral foramen (shaft)
Radius, proximal	Ulnar facets (articular end), posterolateral foramen (shaft)
Radius, distal	Articular end, unlar fusion facet (shaft)
Metacarpal, proximal	Carpal 2+3 facet (articular end)
Metacarpal, distal	Distal condyles (articular end)
Femur, proximal	Head (articular end), anterior nutrient foramen (shaft)
Femur, distal	Articular end, supracondyloid fossa (shaft)
Tibia, proximal	Intercondylor fossa (articular end), posterolateral foramen (shaft)
Tibia, distal	Articular end
Calcaneus	Tarsal C+4 facet
Metatarsal, proximal	Tarsal 2+3 facet (articular end)
Metatarsal, distal	Distal condyles (articular end)
First Phalanx	Proximal articular end, distal articular end
Second Phalanx	Proximal articular end, distal articular end

have a major and often unappreciated effect on subsequent attempts at quantification (see Lyman 1994a: 102-104).

Like the MNI, the MNE is a derived measure, an estimate, in this case of the minimum number of some specific element (mandibles, for instance) which could be represented in the sample of generally fragmentary specimens in a faunal assemblage. It is of course specific to a particular taxon, most appropriately a particular species. It is also an estimate based on a count. The question is, what do we count?

If the assemblage consisted entirely of complete bones we could simply count them, and our estimate would be exact. But most archaeological assemblages encompass some degree of breakage, and the more breakage the more difficult the estimate. Inevitably, particular portions of the element are counted, and in practise these "counting portions" have tended to be relatively few in number. Judging from observed practise and a few published sources (e.g. Klein and Cruz-Uribe 1984), it seems that longbones are usually counted at the proximal and distal ends, innominates at the acetabulum, scapula at the distal end, ribs

Table 3.3. Faunal remains by vertebrate class.

	Bison Skull East		Bison Skull West		Rita-Claire	
	f	%	f	%	f	%
Mammal	1073	80.8	967	93.0	9378	72.2
Bird	247	18.6	72	6.9	3188	24.5
Fish	8	0.6	1	0.1	427	3.3
Subtotal	1328	100.0	1040	100.0	12993	100.0
Class uncertain	0		0		48	
Total	1328		1040		13041	

at the proximal end, vertebrae at the centrum or neural canal, and mandibles at the mental foramen, the mandibular condyle and/or a particular tooth socket.

If the assemblage is not too fragmented, this system can work quite well. For the Rita-Claire and Bison Skull assemblages it provided results which could not be improved upon for all taxa except caribou. But here, large and highly fragmented assemblages meant that counting at different portions yielded sometimes quite different results. To take one of the more extreme examples, the MNE for proximal femurs from Rita-Claire is 11 counting on proximal articular ends, and 24 counting at the anterior proximal foramen. Articular-end destruction is common in many large-mammal faunal assemblages (see Todd and Rapson 1988, Lyman 1994a: 266ff), so that articular-end counts are often of dubious value. Marean and Spencer (1991) suggest on the basis of experimental studies that mid-shaft counts provide the most reliable MNE estimates for ravaged assemblages, but recognition problems and the absence of useable counting portions frustrated attempts to base longbone counts on mid-shafts.

Morlan (1994) has defined element portions suitable for calculating MNEs for bison, most of which can be directly transferred to caribou or any other large to medium-sized mammal. Not all are suitable for every type of study, however. As Morlan (1994: 799) discusses, some portions are relatively discrete, readily identifiable anatomical features, such as nutrient foramen or muscle attachment marks. Others are large, vaguely defined zones, recognizable by their size and general configuration. The posterior

shaft of the metatarsal would be an example. The distinction is not a rigorous one, but it does have a practical application. Calculating MNEs using non-discrete portions requires the "hands on" matching of fragments (see Ringrose 1993:130), while discrete portions in at least the great majority of cases can simply be counted. For large collections and situations where lay-out space is limited this is major advantage, for it means that MNEs can be directly calculated from a computer database.

Unfortunately, not all elements are well endowed with discrete, countable features, and not all are situated so as to be useful. If one is already counting metatarsals using the proximal articular end, the addition of the adjacent posterior nutrient foramen does not yield much new information, since it too close to the proximal end to be usually independent of it. A similar situation pertains to the distal metatarsal and both ends of the metacarpus, while the distal tibia lacks any clear, discrete features above the articular end.

The counting features or portions used in this study are presented in Table 3.2. They do not exhaust the list of possibilities, and could quite likely be improved upon. They were chosen with the desire of sampling both articular ends and adjacent shaft portions, and make distinctions based on commonly observed fracture patterns. Thus the articular end of the distal tibia is counted as a unit since it is rarely if ever broken longitudinally. This is not true of the proximal femur, where the counting feature is specifically the ball or head. Not included here are the many small elements such as the carpals and tarsals (excluding the calcaneus) which are almost

Table 3.4. Vertebrate remains from Bison Skull East.

Taxon	Common name	NISP	%NISP	MNI	%MNI
Bony Fishes					
Coregoninae subfamily	whitefish/inconnu	8	100.0	2	100
Total fishes		8			
Birds					
Gavia immer/adamsii	common/yellow-billed loon	1	0.5	1	4.3
C. columbianus/buccinator	tundra/trumpeter swan	10	5.4	1	4.3
Anserini tribe	goose	79	42.7	9	39.1
Anatinae subfamily	duck	42	22.7	7	30.4
Anatidae family	duck/goose	11	5.9		
Lagopus lagopus/mutus	willow/rock ptarmigan	39	21.1	4	17.4
Larus hyperboreus	glacous gull	2	1.1	1	4.3
Larus sp.	gull	1	0.5		
Total identified bird		185	100.0	23	100.0
Class Aves	unidentified bird	62			
Total birds		247			
Mammals					
Rangifer tarandus	caribou	624	98.58	10	62.5
Canis sp.	dog or wolf	1	0.16	1	6.25
Ondatra zibethicus	muskrat	1	0.16	1	6.25
Phoca hispida	ringed seal	4	0.63	1	6.25
Erignathus barbatus	bearded seal	1	0.16	1	6.25
Cetacea	unidentified whale	1	0.16	1	6.25
Microtus oeconomus	tundra vole	1	0.16	1	6.25
Total identified mammal		633	100.00	16	100.00
Class Mammalia	unidentified mammal	168			
Class Mammalia	mammal size 3	5			
Class Mammalia	mammal size 4	1			
Class Mammalia	mammal size 5	266			
Total mammals		1073			
Total vertebrates		1328			

always found complete or nearly so, or the various cranial elements which while recorded were not counted for MNE purposes.

MNEs were based on direct counts of these portions. In the case of elements where more than one portion is listed, the MNE is equal to the largest result. Except for purposes of MNI calculation, side was not considered, nor was age or size, except in certain circumstances. For various analytical reasons, it was sometimes felt appropriate to distinguish between juvenile and non-juvenile elements, so that separate MAU tables could be calculated for each.

An Overview of the Faunal Assemblages

Basic descriptive data for the three site components arranged by vertebrate class are presented in Table 3.3 and expanded in Tables 3.4 to 3.6.

Fish Remains

The Rita-Claire and Bison Skull fish bone assemblages are limited in both size and diversity (Tables 3.4-3.6). Bison Skull, particularly, produced no more than a handful of fish remains, nine specimens in all, divided

Table 3.5. Vertebrate remains from Bison Skull West.

Taxon	Common name	NISP	%NISP	MNI	%MNI
Bony Fishes					
Coregoninae subfamily	whitefish/inconnu	1	100.0	1	100
Total fishes		1			
Birds					
C. columbianus/buccinator	tundra/trumpeter swan	10	25.6	1	12.5
Anserini tribe	goose	21	53.8	3	37.5
Anatinae subfamily	duck	3	7.7	2	25
Lagopus lagopus/mutus	willow/rock ptarmigan	5	12.8	2	25
Total identified birds		39	100.0	8	100
Class Aves	unidentified bird	33			
Total birds		72			
Mammals					
Ovibos moschatus	muskox	4	0.6	1	4.8
Large artiodactyl	cf. moose/muskox	1	0.1		
Rangifer tarandus	caribou	707	98.6	17	81.0
Phoca hispida	ringed seal	3	0.4	1	4.8
Cetacea	unidentified whale	1	0.1	1	4.8
Rodentia	size 1 rodent	1	0.1	1	4.8
Total identified mammal		717	100.0	21	100.0
Class Mammalia	unident. mammal	104			
Class Mammalia	mammal size 5	146			
Total mammals		967			
Total vertebrates		1040			

between the two components. The Rita-Claire sample, with 427 specimens, is still comparatively small. As Table 3.6 details, *Gadidae* (cod) bone was the most common by a considerable margin, representing over 70% of NISPs and 60% of MNIs. In most or all cases this cod is probably to be identified with burbot (*Lota lota*). The whitefish subfamily (*Coregoninae*), including both whitefish (*Coregonus* spp.) and inconnu (*Stenodus leucichthys*), are the next most abundant, and except for a few sculpin bones may represent all of the remainder of the sample. Only whitefish were represented at Bison Skull.

In the 20th century, the lower Horton Channel - Harrowby Bay area was considered to be generally poor in fish resources, with clear, sediment-free waters which made netting unproductive (Mackay 1958: 115). Fish remains and fishing gear at Bison Skull and Rita-Claire are few enough that most or all may have been brought in from some other

location in the local seasonal round.

Bird Remains

Bird remains were few in number and limited in diversity at Bison Skull (Tables 3.4 and 3.5). However, almost 25% of the Rita-Claire faunal material was assignable to a very considerable range of avian taxa (Table 3.6). Almost all are waterfowl, with geese and ducks together accounting for 88.9% of avian NISPs and 79.5% of MNIs. Although quantification procedures may differ somewhat, it seems that waterfowl remains were more abundant at Rita-Claire than any other Inuvialuit archaeological site for which there are detailed faunal estimates (Morrison 1988, 1990, 1994; Nagy 1990; Balkwill 1987; Swayze 1994; Balkwill and Rick 1994). As has been discussed, no attempt was made during analysis to distinguish the various duck or geese species; had this been done the MNI totals would have been even larger. Important

Table 3.6. Vertebrate remains from Rita-Claire.

Taxon	Common name	NISP	%NISP	MNI	%MNI
Bony Fishes					
Coregoninae subfamily	whitefish/inconnu	41	19.2	7	35
Salmonidae family	whitefish/trout	9	4.2		
Gadidae family	cod	156	73.2	12	60
Cottidae family	sculpin	7	3.3	1	5
Total identified fish		213	100.0	20	100
Unidentified fish		214			
Total fishes		427			
Birds					
Gavia stellata/pacifica	red-throated/Pacific loon	6	0.3	2	1.1
Gavia immer/adamsii	common/yellow-billed loon	6	0.3	3	1.6
Gavia sp.	loon	7	0.4		
Podiceps grisegena	red-necked grebe	1	0.1	1	0.5
Cygnus columbianus	tundra swan	8	0.4	2	1.1
C. columbianus/buccinator	tundra/trumpeter swan	3	0.2		
Anserini tribe	goose	867	43.7	79	42.7
Anserinae subfamily	swan/goose	8	0.4		
Anatinae subfamily	duck	855	43.1	68	36.8
Anatidae family	duck/goose	42	2.1		
Lagopus lagopus/mutus	willow/rock ptarmigan	153	7.7	19	10.3
Stercorarius sp.	jaeger	2	0.1	1	0.5
Larus sp.	gull	2	0.1	1	0.5
Laridae family	jaeger/gull/tern	15	0.8	5	2.7
Charadriidae/Scolopacidae	plover/sandpipers	4	0.2	2	1.1
Charadniformes order	shore bird	5	0.3	1	0.5
cf. *Nyctea scandiaca*	probable snowy owl	1	0.1	1	0.5
Total identified bird		1985	100.0	185	100.0
Class Aves		1203			
Total birds		3188			

local species include scaup (*Aythya spp.*), oldsquaw (*Clangula hyemalis*), common eider (*Somateria mollissima*), snow geese (*Chen caerulescens*), white-fronted goose (*Anser albifrons*, locally known as "yellow legs"), and Canada goose (*Branta canadensis*) (Martell et al. 1984; Godfrey 1986).

A high proportion of avian longbones (more than 80%) are represented by diastema shafts without the proximal and distal ends. The ends of the longbone shafts often had a torn or shredded appearance, possibly due to organic degradation in what appears to be a fairly acidic soil matrix. About 10% of the avian bone was identified as coming from juvenile individuals.

Mammal Bone

Many thousands of mammal bones were recovered from the Rita-Claire and Bison Skull sites. Analysis focusses only on excavated specimens; the two muskox and single bison skull found semi-buried in the eastern component of the Bison Skull site, and the 53 caribou skulls arranged in a line down the slope at the Rita-Claire site, are *not* included. As with the bird and fish remains, the mammal bones have been sorted into taxonomic categories as appropriate (Tables 3.4-3.6).

The mammalian fauna from all three site components is very heavily dominated by caribou bone. The two Bison Skull

Table 3.6 (continued).

Taxon	Common name	NISP	%NISP	MNI	%MNI
Mammals					
Alces alces	moose	1	0.03	1	2.1
Ovibos moschatus	muskox	6	0.18	1	2.1
Large artiodactyl	cf. moose/muskox	5	0.15		
Rangifer tarandus	caribou	3206	95.90	26	54.2
Ursus sp.	unidentified bear	1	0.03	1	2.1
Canis cf. *familiarus*	small canid (dog?)	1	0.03	1	2.1
Canis cf. *lupus*	large canid (wolf?)	1	0.03	1	2.1
Canis sp.	unidentified canid	2	0.06		
Alopex lagopus	arctic fox	22	0.66	6	12.5
Vulpes vulpes	red fox	3	0.09	1	2.1
Alopex/Vulpes	unidentified fox	15	0.45		
Lynx lynx	lynx	1	0.03	1	2.1
Ondatra zibethicus	muskrat	4	0.12	3	6.3
Spermophilus parryi	groundsquirrel	8	0.24	2	4.2
Phoca hispida	ringed seal	61	1.82	2	4.2
Erignathus barbatus	bearded seal	4	0.12	1	2.1
Delphinapterus leucas	beluga whale	1	0.03	1	2.1
Cetacea	unidentified whale	1	0.03		
Total identified mammals		3343		48	100.0
Class Mammalia	unident. mammal	2511			
Class Mammalia	mammal size 2	10			
Class Mammalia	mammal size 3	55			
Class Mammalia	mammal size 4	53			
Class Mammalia	mammal size 5	3406			
Total mammals		9378			
Total vertebrates		12993			

components are nearly identical, with caribou accounting for over 98% of mammalian NISPs, and a handful of other species represented by four or fewer specimens each. "Minority" species include two large artiodactyls - moose and muskox - ringed seal, bearded seal, muskrat, and canid. Small slivers of cetacean bone may represent tool-making debitage, while a lone tundra vole specimen (the maxillary portion of a rostrum) is probably non-cultural in origin. The absence of identified bison bone and near absence of muskox bone suggest that the bison and two muskox skulls found at Bison Skull East do not represent simple butchering detritus. If the people who hunted at the Bison Skull site did kill a bison, they did not kill it at the site, nor did they butcher it there.

It can be noted that the species list is slightly more diverse at the look-out/shooting-blind portion of the site (Bison Skull East) than in the bone bed (Bison Skull West). It is perhaps surprising, in light of the functions inferred for these two areas, that any non-caribou bone was found at all, particularly in the bone bed. It can only be suggested that small quantities of non-caribou food may have been consumed while people were waiting for or butchering caribou. Possibly, too, one or both site areas include small, unrecognized habitation components.

The range of "minority" species is considerably greater at the Rita-Claire habitation site, and a few present some interesting anomalies. Muskrat and especially arctic fox are represented by unusually high MNI figures considering their low NISP values. Compared with, for instance, seals,

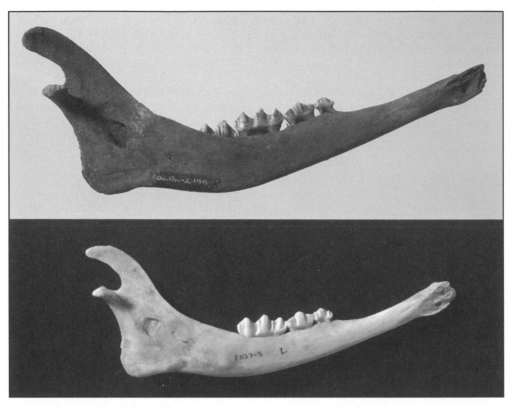

Figure 3.1. Upper: Juvenile caribou mandible, with m1 erupting, Rita-Claire site; Lower: July-killed comparative specimen (CMC collections, catalogue F1137-5).

both fox and muskrat are represented by only a very limited number of anatomical elements, particularly, in both cases, mandibles. This may reflect a distinctive possibly non-food use for these two species, or perhaps taphonomic histories which differ from those of other species remains. These very high MNI/NISP ratios have a clear effect on relative caribou frequencies, depressing a %NISP of 95.9% to a %MNI of only 54.2%.

Only one species at the Rita-Claire site is out of its modern range; the lynx, an animal normally associated with the northern boreal forest. However it is represented by only a single claw sheath, and likely represents a non-food item, possibly introduced into the site as part of a piece of fur clothing or trim.

It is difficult to suggest which other minority species were hunted from the site, and which may have been brought in as provisions from elsewhere (cf. Gronnow et al. 1983: 69-70). Beluga and other cetaceans are not available in the immediate site area, while seals seem also to be relatively rare, even in Harrowby Bay (Mackay 1958: 115; Freeman 1976: 10). They may have been brought in from elsewhere, possibly as whole carcasses in the case of the seals (with their low MNI/NISP ratio). Moose and muskox may have been hunted from the site, but if so it must have been on a very casual basis, to judge by the infrequency of their remains.

Seasonality

The use of faunal remains to determine the season or seasons during which a site was occupied is a longstanding tradition in archaeology, but one which must be approached with some caution. Particularly in the Arctic, the ease with which food may be stored from one season to the next can greatly hamper interpretation. Waterfowl are a case in point. They are found in far northern latitudes only during the brief open-water season - approximately May through September - but their remains appear in most or all Inuvialuit archaeological sites, even the most winter oriented (e.g. Morrison 1990: Table 1). Clearly, at least in the case of winter sites (where stored food was often a staple), it cannot be assumed that there is always an immediate relationship between the season when an animal was killed and the season when it was eaten and its remains deposited in an archaeological site.

With this caveat in mind, we can turn to the estimation of the season or seasons during which the Rita-Claire and Bison Skull sites were occupied. The absence of winter housing points immediately to a relatively warm-season occupation, sometime between about May and late October. This period can be narrowed down greatly with respect to the associated faunal material.

The heavy focus on caribou hunting provides a background to any interpretation. As we have seen, caribou were hunted primarily during the autumn or late summer/autumn almost everywhere in the Inuit world, when hides were prime and animals fattest. But some caribou hunting did occur in the spring and early summer as well, and at least one early-season caribou-hunting site has been identified archaeologically from the Inuvialuit area (Nagy 1990). Several observations, however, tie the Rita-Claire/Bison Skull hunt firmly to the autumn season.

One of these is the age of the young caribou calves found in all of the assemblages. The Rita-Claire site produced an MNI of five caribou under one year of age, represented by right mandibles. All had their first molars erupting, indicating an age of about three to five months, and a death - considering an early

June birth - anytime from about early September through early November (Fig. 3.1). Entirely absent were animals with no first molar eruption (indicating a summer death), with a first molar which was fully erupted but no evidence of a second molar (indicating a winter death), or with the second molar erupting (which would suggest the spring or early summer death of animals at or just under one year of age). Two individuals are represented with m2 fully erupted and no m3 eruption, indicating a death with outside limits at 12 and 22 months of age, but most probably between 15 and 17 months or, again, between early September and early November, in this case of their second year. The eruption of m3 shows too much variation between individuals to be useful in establishing season of death (see Miller 1974: Table 4 for caribou dental eruption sequences).

The two Bison Skull components present a similar picture. Bison Skull East yielded a mandibular MNI of two juvenile individuals with m1 erupting, and one individual with m2 fully erupted and an m3 which has *just* broken the bone (but certainly not the gum line). Bison Skull West yielded only a single juvenile specimen with m1 erupting, although many others were observed in the unexcavated, surface area of the bone bed. Specimens in which m1 was fully erupted, or with m2 in eruption, were absent.

There is some reason to suspect a particular focus - although probably not an exclusive one - on the early half of this autumn season. Antler from all three components seemed typically to be in a velvet state indicating, if this identification is correct (and there are no tested criteria for identifying velvet antler in an archaeological context), that most animals had been killed before the end of September (see Kelsall 1968: 39-40). The evidence of hide staking at Bison Skull East also supports an occupation relatively early in the autumn, when hides were still thin enough to be useful for clothing.

The abundant bird bone - particularly at Rita-Claire - also suggests an early autumn

Figure 3.2. Waterfowl are abundant in the Old Horton Channel/Harrowby Bay area.

season. Medullary bone is a secondary calcium deposit present in the bones of reproductively active female birds, and in the Arctic can generally be taken to indicate a late spring or early summer (May or June) season of death (Rick 1975). Only one specimen exhibiting medullary bone was recovered from the Rita-Claire site - a (probable) snowy owl tibiotarsus - and none from Bison Skull. It seems unlikely, then, that waterfowl were being hunted from the sites during the late May-June breeding season, presumably because the sites were not occupied at the time. On the other hand, high frequencies of waterfowl bone, including juvenile waterfowl bone, from Rita-Claire point to a significant hunt later in the season, but again before the end of September, when waterfowl have migrated south. At present, the Harrowby Bay - lower Old Horton Channel area is a "critical" summer moulting and early autumn staging location for waterfowl (Fig. 3.2), particularly geese (Martell et al. 1984: Fig. 5, Table 4). While caribou hunting seems to have been the main economic focus, the seasonally very abundant local waterfowl were evidently not neglected.

Only fish remains present a possibly ambiguous picture of seasonal exploitation. The Rita-Claire fish assemblage — small as it is — is dominated by cod remains, probably representing burbot. Other Inuvialuit archaeological fish-bone assemblages tend to be not only relatively larger and more diverse, but show a different composition. Most exhibit a clear preponderance of whitefish remains, with cod or burbot running a distant second, third, or fourth (e.g. Morrison 1988: Tables 7 and 8, 1994: Table 1; Swayze 1994: Table 1; Balkwill and Rick 1994: Fig. 2), the reverse of the situation at Rita-Claire.

Unfortunately it is very difficult to interpret this contrast in the light of known seasonal variation in the availablity of different fish species. On one hand, burbot is the only common fish in the western Arctic which spawns under the ice of early winter (Scott and Crossman 1973: 644), and it has been suggested that it may have often formed the mainstay of the traditional winter fishery (Morrison 1988: 69; Balkwill and Rick 1994: 113; see also Stefansson 1962: 359). Yet the Rita-Claire site lacks architectural or any other evidence of a winter occupation. Western Arctic fish resources have been very little studied outside of the immediate Mackenzie-Arctic Red River drainage (Martell et al 1984), and it may be that, relative to whitefish, burbot are simply more common in this area than in many others. There is also the possibility that all or part of the unusually small fish-bone assemblages from all three components was brought in from elsewhere.

The Structure of the Caribou Assemblages

Introduction

Caribou bone makes up the great majority of mammalian remains at Rita-Claire and Bison Skull, and is the focus of analysis for the rest of this study. In Chapter 4, patterns of fragmentation and taphonomic and other factors affecting the representation of various anatomical elements are investigated. Some of the results are more descriptive than strictly analytical, but are presented for comparative purposes. The analysis of caribou-bone assemblages from the Arctic lags far behind that of bison in Plains assemblages - the other major area of North America where a large herd animal formed a fairly consistent basis of subsistence - in both methodological rigour and interpretative results (e.g. Wilson 1980; Speth 1983; Frison and Todd 1987). The following discussions are presented with a view to advancing interpretations of caribou use at two archaeological sites on the Cape Bathurst Peninsula. They are also presented in the hope that by providing comparative data and exploring the usefulness of various analytical tests (many of them derived from bison studies) they can help advance the interpretation of caribou faunas in general.

Part I: Fragmentation and Density-Mediated Destruction

Percent Complete

Much of the caribou bone at the Rita-Claire and Bison Skull sites was broken. To investigate fragmentation patterns, MNEs were calculated for each anatomical part. Percentages of complete bones per MNE were then determined (cf. Todd and Rapson 1988: 308-309), and graphed as Figure 4.1. As can be seen, all three components present distribution curves which seem to be variations on a common theme. All exhibit relatively high percentages of complete vertebrae, carpals, and tarsals, and much lower percentages of complete long bones, with mandibles, ribs, scapulae, innominates, and to some extent phalanges occupying a variable middle ground. In other words, linear-shaped bones with significant marrow cavities tend to be fragmented, and small, compact, non-marrow bones tend to be relatively complete. A similar breakage "signature" is probably characteristic of most caribou and other size class 5 mammal bone assemblages.

What is variable is the amplitude of breakage. Fragmentation is much more extensive at the Rita-Claire habitation site than at Bison Skull East (the look-out/kill area) and particularly Bison Skull West (the bone bed). Overall, at Rita-Claire complete or essentially complete bones constitute 53.8% of total MNEs; at Bison Skull East the figure is 58.6%; while 73.9% of Bison Skull West MNEs are complete. A few particular elements seem to reflect best this amplitude shift, including mandibles (where %complete ranges from 6.4% [Rita-Claire] to 60% [Bison Skull West]), innominates (7.1% to 57.1%), ribs (38.9% to 54.8%), and scapulae (43.5% to 95.8%). The long bones are also illuminating. As in many assemblages (e.g. Morrison 1988; Stenton 1989: 277), complete caribou long bones are absent from both Rita-Claire and Bison Skull East, a single juvenile radius from Rita-Claire being the lone exception. Yet complete specimens of all three fore-limb elements are well represented at Bison Skull West, including humeri (40% complete), radii (50% complete), and ulnae (36.4 % complete). Even at Bison Skull West,

percent complete

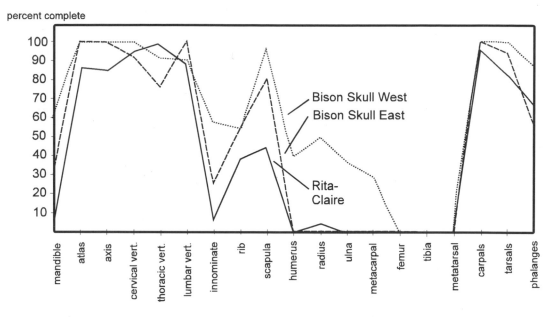

Figure 4.1. Percent complete.

however, none of the hind limb bones was complete.

Splinters and Shaft Cylinders

Binford (1981) has proposed several tests which can be used to assess bone fragmentation. One is based on the observation that carnivore gnawing tends to reduce longbones to shaft cylinders and then to splinters. Longbone splinters per MNI are plotted against shaft cylinders per MNI (Binford 1981: Fig. 4.60) to investigate the possibility that carnivore gnawing might be a significant causal factor in the formation of the bone assemblage. Wolf-kill faunas plotted for these variables display a characteristic V-shape: the number of cylinders rises and then decreases as the number of splinters rises. In other words, long bones are gnawed to produce both cylinders and splinters, but as the gnawing continues the cylinders themselves are reduced to splinters. Applying this model to Rita-Claire and Bison Skull requires the assumption that all (or at least the great majority) of size class 5 mammal long bone splinters can be assigned to caribou; a

reasonable assumption considering the overall makeup of the assemblages. The resulting figures are placed into Binford's matrix in Figure 4.2.

Results are consistent with those obtained with %complete. Bison Skull West is the least fragmented, with very low cylinders/MNI and splinters/MNI ratios (0.2 and 7.5 respectively). Rita-Claire is by far the most fragmented, with a moderately elevated shaft cylinders/MNI ratio (1.6), and a dramatically higher splinters/MNI ratio (100.6). Bison Skull East falls in between, but closer to Bison Skull West. For comparative purposes, caribou-bone ratios from Kugaluk, a mid-19th century Inuvialuit occupation site (Morrison 1988: Fig. 24), are also included. They are very similar to those from Rita-Claire.

Despite these consistencies, the use of splinter and cylinder ratios to assess fragmentation presents a number of problems. One is the manner in which splinters are counted. As discussed, in faunas heavily dominated by a single prey species, it seems reasonable to assume that all longbone shaft

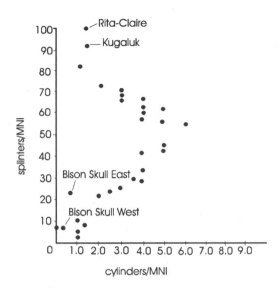

Figure 4.2. Relationship between number of long bone splinters and cylinders per MNI (after Binford: 1981: Fig. 4.60).

splinters of a suitable curvature and cortical thickness can be assigned to that species (at least for purposes of the test). Yet in highly fragmented assemblages many shaft splinters may be so comminuted that they cannot be easily recognized as such.

Perhaps more serious is the problem of sample size. It seems likely that splinter and cylinder frequencies will increase much more rapidly than MNI as sample size increases, in the same way and for the same reasons that NISP increases more rapidly than MNI (see Grayson 1984). Thus small samples will tend to fall toward the apparently pristine, unravaged end of the graph regardless of the intensity of fragmentation, while most (but not all; see Speth 1983: Fig. 22) large samples will appear ravaged. It can be noted from Figure 4.2 that the degree of ravaging among the study assemblages does appear to be correlated with sample size (Kugaluk produced almost 24,000 caribou bones [Morrison 1988: Table 6]).

Percent Difference

Another technique for investigating

fragmentation proposed by Binford (1981: Fig. 5.07-5.08) is based on differential destruction of the articular ends of the humerus and tibia. Proximal and distal-end frequencies of both elements show marked differences in survival potential. Binford (1981) suggests that plotting the frequency of proximal vs. distal ends can provide an indication of the intensity of damage. Assemblages with large numbers of distal ends and few proximal ends fall within a "zone of destruction," while assemblages where frequencies are more balanced should be more pristine.

Todd and Rapson (1988; see also Richardson 1980) have taken this idea one step further. They propose a value known as percent difference (%difference) which makes it possible to diagram the degree of damage to both the humerus and the tibia in a single plot. Percent difference is the difference between the number of proximal ends and the number of distal ends (including completes), multiplied by 100 and divided by the sum of both:
%difference = [(complete + proximal) - (complete + distal)] * 100 / [(complete + proximal) + (complete + distal)]

Percent difference tibae vs. %difference humeri for several sites is presented in Figure 4.3 (adapted from Todd and Rapson 1988: Fig. 3). A fairly clear pattern of destruction seems apparent, with %difference tibae increasing together with %difference humeri along a curved or geometric regression line. Five Plains bison-kill sites occupy the base of the chart (Olsen-Chubbuck, Casper, Horner II, Lamb Springs, and Jones-Miller), where articular-end destruction is light to moderate. A group of caribou wolf-kills shows increased destruction, while at the upper end of the chart is a Plains occupation site (Bugas-Holding), where sheep and bison bone was highly fragmented.

The Rita-Claire site is also plotted. It falls well off the regression line, in a zone of moderate destruction greater than that of the bison kill sites, but much less than that of the single Plains occupation site. Neither Bison

Table 4.1. Percent differences: the Rita-Claire and Bison Skull sites.

%difference	Rita-Claire	Bison Skull East	Bison Skull West
humeri	-45.9	-50.0	14.3
tibae	-38.5	5.3	-33.3

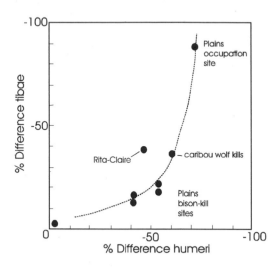

Figure 4.3. Percent difference tibiae vs. percent difference humeri.

Skull East nor Bison Skull West, however, could be plotted, because of the basic assumptions on which the graph is based. Binford's original "zones of destruction" were based on the observation that distal ends survive in greater frequencies than proximal ends under conditions of articular end destruction. Todd and Rapson seem to ignore this issue of directionality, perhaps because all of their examples vary in the expected direction, with distal ends outnumbering proximal ones, yielding a negative %difference result. This is not the case with the two Bison Skull components, where in one case proximal tibae outnumber distal tibia, and in the other, where proximal humeri outnumber distal humeri (Table 4.1). In short, %difference does not offer many clear insights into fragmentation patterns at these sites, beyond the already well-attested observation that the Rita-Claire assemblage is the most fragmented.

Note that juvenile elements were excluded in determining %differences , since they are subject to different survival potentials than the bones of mature animals (Munson 1991).

Destruction of Articular Ends

Percent difference examines articular-end destruction through a rather indirect route, and depends on the assumption that differences in proximal- and distal-end frequencies are due solely to destruction and not differential transport (tibae and humeri need not have been brought to the site as whole bones). A more direct technique used by Todd (1987) and Todd and Rapson (1988) plots frequencies of specific longbone "counting features" along a vertical profile. These features include not only articular ends but also adjacent, discrete shaft portions. Situations where articular ends are under-represented in relation to the adjacent shaft strongly suggest articular end destruction (see Lyman 1994a: 267-271).

Plots of femora and humeri from Rita-Claire show significant under-representation of articular ends (Fig. 4.4 and 4.5). Both Bison Skull components present straighter frequency profiles, with Bison Skull West, in particular, exhibiting no apparent articular end destruction. Todd and Rapson (1988: Fig. 10) graph bison longbone profiles from the Bugas-Holding site which are more extreme but otherwise essentially similar to those Rita-Claire. They also present a humerus profile on caribou bone from one of Binford's (1978) Nunamiut sites (Palangana), which shows the same pattern but to an even more marked degree. In both cases the destruction of articular ends seems to have been due mainly to the manufacture of bone grease.

Structural Density

A quality of many kinds of bone destruction, including organic decomposition

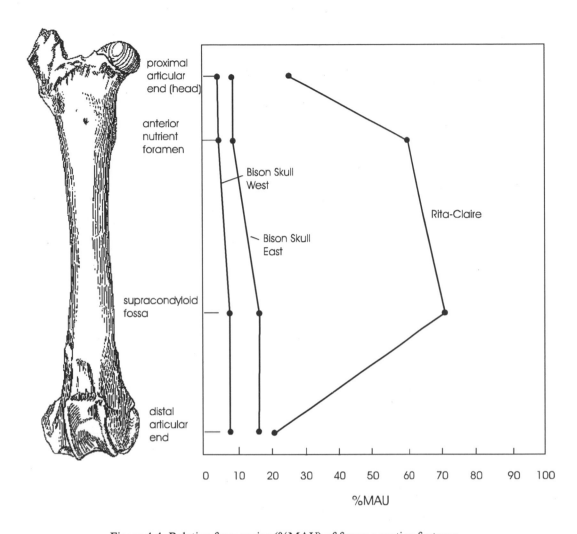

Figure 4.4. Relative frequencies (%MAU) of femur counting features.

and carnivore gnawing, is that it is density-mediated; that is the denser the element the less destruction it suffers (Binford and Bertram 1977; Lyman 1984, 1985). Plotting the relative frequency of anatomical parts against structural density (Lyman 1984, 1994a: 234-258) should reveal either a positive correlation, suggesting that destruction has occurred, or no correlation at all (see Lyman 1991: Figure 3).

Relative frequency is calculated in terms of the %MAU, or "normed minimal animal unit" (Binford 1978, 1984; see also Lyman 1994a: 249, 255). Structural densities are taken from Lyman's (1984) study of deer-bone (*Odocoileus*) densities, which are assumed to be comparable to caribou. Lyman scanned 93 bone sites to determine densities, a list which was later reduced to 33 (Lyman 1984: Table 10). MNEs ("minimum number of elements") and then MAUs were determined for each of these scan sites by counting discrete portions or features at or immediately adjacent to the scan site (see Table 4.2). MAUs were then converted to %MAUs by

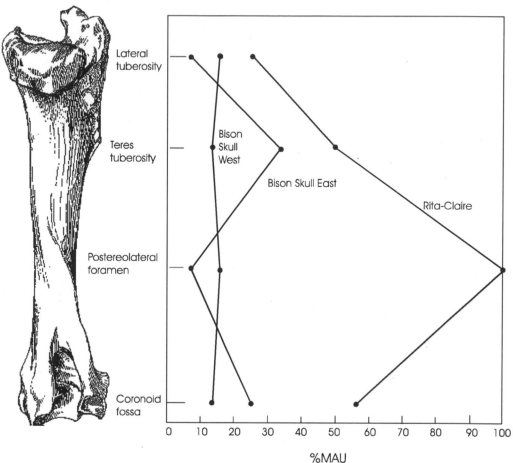

Figure 4.5. Relative frequencies (%MAU) of humerus counting features.

expressing the results as a percentage of the greatest single MAU in the sequence.

Determining %MAUs and densities for specific landmarks or portions of bones is a little more comprehensive and much more precise than the more commonly used method, where anatomical elements like the distal humerus and the innominate are considered as complete units (e.g. Morrison 1988: Fig. 25; Le Blanc 1994: Fig. 18; see also Morlan 1994). However, because the scan sites used for structural density are not necessarily the most abundant portion for each element, the resulting sets of %MAUs are independent of and somewhat different from %MAUs calculated for other purposes. For example, in

the Rita-Claire assemblage a %MAU of 100% was obtained on the mandible, counting at the mental foramen, and the distal humerus, counting at the postereolateral foramen. Neither of these counting features, however, corresponds to a scan site, so that for purposes of comparison with density the mandible figure is reduced to 86.2% (counting at m3) and the distal humerus to 62.1% (counting at the articular end), while it is now the distal metacarpal which achieves a %MAU of 100%.

Two of Lyman's scan sites were not associated with any counting feature noted during analysis, so that the mid-pubis and sternal midline (PU1 and ST1 in his

Table 4.2. Bone density and frequency in the study assemblages.

Scan site	Element/Portion	Rita-Claire %MAU*	Bison Skull East %MAU*	Bison Skull West %MAU*	Density
dn5	mandible: post. alveolus, m3	86.2	72.7	16.7	0.36
at1	atlas: posterior zygapophyses	48.3	54.5	41.7	0.13
ax1	axis: centrum	48.3	54.5	25.0	0.16
ce1	cervical vertebrae: centrum	31.7	40.0	36.7	0.19
th1	thoracic vertebrae: centrum	51.0	32.7	26.7	0.24
lu1	lumbar vertebrae: centrum	45.5	25.5	35.0	0.29
sc1	sacrum: anterior epiphysis	48.3	18.2	0.0	0.19
ac1	innominate: acetabulum	65.5	27.3	41.7	0.27
il1	ilium: tuber sacrale	96.6	9.1	58.3	0.20
is1	ischium: "rolled edge" ischial border	58.6	9.1	33.3	0.41
ri2	rib: head (articular facet)	71.0	40.0	25.0	0.25
sp1	scapula: neck	62.1	27.3	100.0	0.36
hu1	humerus: prox. articular end	27.6	9.1	16.7	0.24
hu5	humerus: dist. articular end	62.1	27.3	12.5	0.39
ra1	radius: prox. articular end	65.5	54.5	50.0	0.42
ra5	radius: dist. articular end	86.2	63.6	50.0	0.43
mc1	metacarpal: prox. post. foramen	79.3	63.6	25.0	0.56
mc6	metacarpal: distal condyles	100.0	54.5	20.8	0.51
fe2	femur: proximal neck	24.1	18.2	4.2	0.36
fe6	femur: distal articular end	24.1	18.2	8.3	0.28
pa1	patella	51.7	18.2	8.3	0.31
ti1	tibia: proximal articular end	34.5	90.9	8.3	0.30
ti5	tibia: distal articular end	93.1	81.8	16.7	0.50
mr1	metatarsal: proximal end	72.4	100.0	8.3	0.55
mr6	metatarsal: distal condyles	79.3	54.5	29.2	0.50
nc1	naviculo-cuboid	55.2	90.9	0.0	0.39
as1	astragalus	89.7	45.5	4.2	0.47
ca2	calcaneus: articulation facet	69.0	72.7	8.3	0.64
p11	first phalanges	86.9	14.5	16.7	0.36
p21	second phalanges	66.2	23.6	19.2	0.28
p31	third phalanges	31.7	1.8	11.7	0.25
*Spearman's rank order correlation with density		0.5413	0.4603	-0.2194	
Significance of Correlation		<0.01	<0.01	>0.05	

* juvenile elements excluded

terminology) had to be dropped from this study because they could not be tabulated properly. Note also that juvenile caribou bone is excluded, since it has different density properties from adult caribou bone. Results are tabulated in Table 4.2.

Spearman's rank order correlations (Siegel 1956) between structural density and MAU follow the same patterns we have already seen in other studies. Both the Rita-Claire and Bison Skull East assemblages are very highly and positively correlated with density (significance <0.01), while in the case of the Bison Skull West assemblage the correlation is negative and insignificant.

Discussion: Processes of Destruction and Fragmentation

Caribou bone from Rita-Claire and Bison Skull exhibits varying degrees of fragmentation and destruction. A number of methods of assessing that fragmentation and destruction have been employed, but as yet the particular agents or processes responsible have not been identified. Many of the tests employed were originally divised with that purpose in mind, yet on further reflection and analysis it becomes apparent that they cannot adequately do so.

Binford's splinter and cylinder ratio test, for instance, assumes that all splinters and cylinders recovered from a site were produced by carnivore gnawing. In situations where we already know this to be true (as in wolf dens), this test might (aside from the problems already discussed) provide an index of the *degree* of ravaging. But for most archaeological purposes it assumes the very thing the archaeologist is trying to determine. Similarly, %difference was designed to measure carnivore destruction, but while it can measure destruction it cannot determine the agent. The Bugas-Holding site provides a good example. It is the "Plains occupation site" appearing at the top end of the chart in Figure 4.3, but here the high degree of tibia and humerus articular end destruction is interpreted by the excavators as primarily the

product of bone grease manufacture, not carnivore gnawing (Todd and Rapson 1988: 313-314).

At the same time, %difference is density-mediated, since both the humerus and the tibia have distal ends which are denser than their proximal ends (Lyman 1984: Table 6). We would thus expect negative %difference results from assemblages which had been subject to any kind of density-mediated destruction. The fact that Bison Skull East produced mixed results (with a positive humerus ratio) despite a highly-significant overall density correlation points out one of the serious limitations of %difference. It is clear and easily graphed, but lacks the comprehensiveness of an overall assemblage comparison with the density index. Without the overall MAU/density comparison we might never suspect that the Bison Skull East assemblage has been significantly altered by density-mediated forces.

Direct comparisons between shaft and articular-end landmarks are another way of looking at bone destruction. At the two Bison Skull components, particularly Bison Skull West, there seems to have been little differential destruction to either articular ends or shafts. At Rita-Claire, however, there has clearly been differential destruction of articular ends. This again, however, is probably density-mediated, at least in part, since longbone ends are generally less dense than shafts.

There are many potential processes of bone fragmentation and destruction. The problem is to get beyond general observations on the degrees of fragmentation and destruction to a better understanding of the specific processes responsible. Several are density-mediated — including carnivore gnawing and organic decomposition — so that tests based on density alone cannot distinguish between them. Others result from deliberate human breakage for a variety of purposes, including butchering, tool manufacture, marrow cracking, and the manufacture of bone grease. And of course relative abundance also reflects human transport decisions to and from a site, again for a variety of purposes. Most of these processes leave definite traces in the bone assemblage, but distinguishing one "signature" from another can often be, as we shall see, problematic.

Part II: Factors Conditioning the Composition of the Caribou Assemblages

Carnivore Tooth-marks

Gnawing produces, in some cases, clear tooth marks on bone. Punctures and pits are easily visible, and the channelling particularly of cancellous bone is also quite distinctive (see Binford 1981: 35-86; Lyman 1994a: 206-212). Clear evidence of carnivore gnawing was observed on 8% of the Rita-Claire caribou bone (n=257), 6.6% of the Bison Skull West caribou bone (n=47), and 4.4% of the caribou bone at Bison Skull East (n=28). Impressionistically, these are not high figures (cf. Lyman 1994a: 276), but comparison is hampered by a lack of reported gnawing frequencies from other caribou assemblages, even those which have been analyzed in some detail (e.g. Gronnow et al. 1983; Stenton 1989). One exception is the Kugaluk site, where "at least 5%" of the caribou bone was determined to have been gnawed (Morrison 1988: 81).

A more insoluble comparative difficulty is the degree of subjectivity involved in identifying gnaw marks, for it seems certain that not all gnawed bone is easily recognizable as such. Criteria applied to the bones from Rita-Claire and Bison Skull (and Kugaluk for that matter) were consistently conservative, identifying only the most obvious examples. Another researcher more familiar with some of the subtler aspects of gnawing might have identified many more examples from the same assemblages. Parenthetically, it can be noted that all of the gnawing observed at the study sites seems to have been produced by a canid-sized carnivore; almost certainly wolf or domestic dog.

Digested bone

Digested bone was identified in the faunal samples by its pitted appearance and reduced density (see Andrews 1990). Like gnawed bone, it is an unambiguous signature of carnivore destruction. The degree of digestion and the large size of the source species (see below) suggest a canid vector, perhaps specifically domestic dog.

Almost all of the digested bone came from Rita-Claire. Seventy isolated specimens were identified, none larger than about 3 cm in any dimension. Twenty-seven could not be identified beyond the Class mammal, 2 were identified as ringed seal, and 39 as caribou. All of the bone identified as caribou consisted of phalanges (first and second), carpals, and tarsals. These (and sesamoids) appear to be the only elements small enough to be ingested whole, and small and compact enough to survive the digestive process in a recognizable form.

Small concentrations of comminuted bone were also encountered at Rita-Claire, all from the same depth (about 25 cm), and in the northwest quadrant of the site (see Fig. 2.20, chapter 2). Where identifiable this bone proved again to be caribou, including the crushed epiphyseal ends of longbones and several phalanges portions. Fragments were typically about fingernail sized or less, and the total weight of the three concentrations was only 135 grams. Many pieces were pitted from digestion; some showed clear tooth marks; and in a few cases microscopic examination revealed adhering fecal material. The presence of this comminuted bone from an otherwise largely sterile area of the site suggests the possibility that it represents part of a dog yard.

No evidence of digested bone was recovered from Bison Skull East. Bison Skull West produced two fragments of digested caribou bone; an intermediate carpal and a second phalanx.

Organic Decomposition and Weathering

Aerial weathering does not appear to have been an important factor affecting the nature or composition of the assemblages from Rita-Claire or Bison Skull. Most excavated bone was in nearly pristine condition, exhibiting no more than a few longitudinal drying cracks, typical of the first of Behrensmeyer's five weathering stages (Behrensmeyer 1978). The occasional specimen found protruding from the sod showed a little more weathering on the protruding portion, typically Stage 2, accompanied by sun bleaching. A notable exception is the bison skull itself, weathered to Stage 3 and patchily to Stage 4 on exposed surfaces. Stage 3-4 weathering also characterizes some of the entirely surficial bone, such as the caribou skulls arranging in a line down the Rita-Claire hillside. None of this surficial bone, however, was collected. The contrast between weathered surficial bone and nearly pristine buried bone suggests that for the most part burial was relatively rapid.

Although evidence of aerial weathering was minor, there was clear evidence of organic decomposition at the Rita-Claire site, in the form of a spongy, wet-cardboard-like texture of many bone specimens. It was accompanied by a tendency for the bone surface to delaminate as it separated from the disintegrating cortex beneath. As already discussed, it is likely that the primary process was demineralization under patchily wet, acidic soil conditions. Nothing comparable was observed at Bison Skull, where soils were well-drained and sandy.

Organic decomposition is, as has been noted, density-mediated, and it seems unarguable that some of the high correlation between the Rita-Claire caribou assemblage and the density index can be attributed to this fact. It is otherwise difficult to quantify this aspect of assemblage destruction, beyond the observation that 1472 mammalian specimens (15.7% of the sample) presented clear evidence of decomposition. Many of the more affected specimens are damaged beyond further identification; thus of the 1472 "decomposed" specimens, 1063 (72.2%) could not be identified beyond the Class level (except in some cases by size). Of the identified caribou bone, 12.6% (n=403) was recognizably decomposed.

Marrow Cracking and Butchering

The Marrow Index

One way of investigating marrow breakage is to compare anatomical part frequencies and a marrow index which measures the potential marrow "utility" for each element. Results should allow an assessment of the importance which the potential marrow yield of each element had in conditioning the overall composition of the assemblage. In other words, the intention is to measure the relationship between utility and differential transport, with the assumption that cracking did not result in the obliteration of faunal elements (see Brink and Dawe 1989: 138-139). The absence of such a relationship, of course, does not preclude marrow cracking, which might still have been practised on an assemblage brought into a site for some other purpose or purposes entirely.

Binford (1978) produced the first marrow index, but it has come under some very pertinent criticism by Jones and Metcalf (1988). They point out that the volume of the marrow cavity alone is the "best" index of utility, without the other variables Binford attempted to factor in (extractive efficiency, % oleic acid). They also suggest that longbones be considered as complete units, rather than as proximal and distal ends as treated by Binford. A new and much simpler index can thus be made by taking the marrow cavity volume in millilitres (Binford 1978: Table 1.6), assigning a value of 1 to elements without a marrow cavity, and collapsing proximal and distal values for longbones (which are identical in any case). A comparison against relative anatomical abundance (%MAU) yields some interesting results (Table 4.3).

The Spearman's Rank Order Correlation between %MAU and the marrow index is

Table 4.3. Spearman's rank order correlation between frequency and the marrow index.

Element	Bison Skull West %MAU*	Bison Skull East %MAU*	Rita-Claire %MAU*	marrow index
skull	25	50	47.1	1
mandible	16.7	100	100	11
atlas	41.7	50	41.2	1
axis	25	50	41.2	1
cervical	36.7	36.7	27.1	1
thorassic	26.3	29.5	43.4	1
lumbar	35	23.3	38.8	1
pelvis	29.2	25	82.4	6
rib	24.7	48.1	60.6	1
sternum	33.3	33.3	41.2	1
scapula	100	25	52.9	5
humerus	16.7	33.3	100	38
radial-ulna	50	58.3	73.5	36
metacarpus	25	58.3	85.3	21
femur	8.3	16.7	70.6	52
tibia	16.7	83.3	79.4	64
calcaneus	8.3	66.7	29.4	3
metatarsus	29.2	91.7	67.6	51
1st phalanges	16.7	12.5	74.3	4
2nd phalanges	18.8	20.8	56.6	2
Correlation coefficient	-0.36	0.22	0.75	
Significance	>0.05	>0.05	<0.01	

* juvenile elements excluded

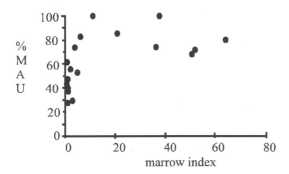

Figure 4.6. Relative frequencies (%MAU) and the marrow index: Rita-Claire site.

positive and strikingly high at Rita-Claire (rho=0.75, p<0.01), negative but just below the 0.05 significance threshold at Bison Skull West (rho=-0.36) and insignificant at Bison Skull East (rho=0.22). Graphing the results (Fig. 4.6) shows a definite threshold effect at Rita-Claire. Here where the marrow index is less than 10 (i.e. elements with a very small or

no marrow cavity) the %MAU is consistently less than 65, and conversely where %MAU is greater than 65 the marrow index is consistently greater than 10. Otherwise, there is relatively little order within the two "clouds" thus distinguished.

Unfortunately, we cannot necessarily conclude that selection for marrow utility was a major factor conditioning the composition of this assemblage, for there is a complication. Speth (1991: 37) has noticed that there is a highly significant (p<0.01) correlation between bulk density and Binford's marrow index. To ascertain if it holds for our new "whole-bone" index as well, a Spearman's Rank Order Correlation was made between it and Lyman's (1984) volume density values. Since many elements, including particularly longbones, were scanned at a number of locations, the density of the complete bone is considered to be the highest value for any of the scanned sites on that element. The results are, again,

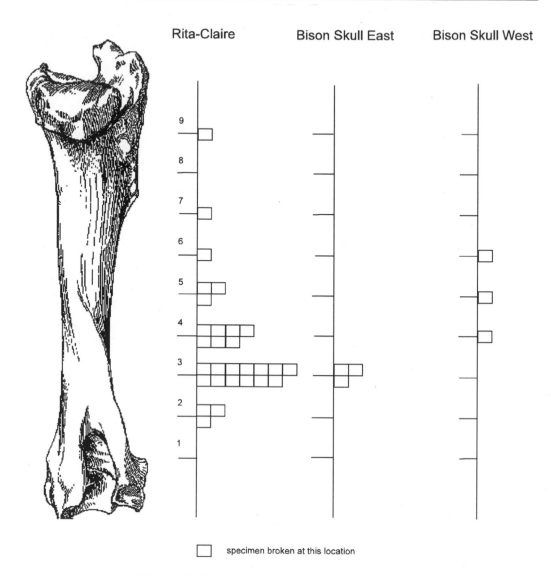

Figure 4.7. Shaft lengths attached to distal humeri.

highly significant (rho=0.86, p<0.01), suggesting that much or all of the high correlation between anatomical frequencies and the marrow index *may* be due to a high correlation with density.

Breakage Locations: Longbones

There is, however, another avenue of investigation open; the analysis of breakage patterns and locations. Binford (1978: 152-

153) records two methods of caribou-bone marrow cracking used by the Nunamiut of north Alaska. One was characteristically employed on upper limb bones, particularly the humerus and femur. These elements were always freed of articulations, cleaned, and then broken by impact at the "neck" immediately below an articular end. By striking at the junction between the dense bone of the shaft and the cancellous bone extending down from the articular end, the marrow has a greater

Figure 4.8. Articulated distal metacarpal,
Rita-Claire, 26 cm depth.

chance of remaining free of bone impact chips (Binford 1981: 158-159). For this reason, "isolated " articular ends with little attached shaft are considered "the exclusive or dominant forms in assemblages cracked for marrow by man" (Binford 1981: 173).

Todd and Rapson (1988) propose a coding system for bison bone which measures the amount of shaft attached to articular ends. It is calculated by dividing the overall length of the specimen by the width at the articular end, yielding a ratio which remains constant from large male to small female specimens. This is an admirable way of dealing with the great sexual dimorphism characteristic of bison. It is not required for caribou, where clearer if slightly less precise results can be obtained by simply estimating the proportion of attached shaft on a consistent scale of 1 to 10. Thus an element coded "d.3" consists of a distal end and shaft amounting to about three-tenths of the overall length of the element. Shaft length estimates were made for all of the articular-end longbone specimens at Rita-Claire and Bison Skull. To ensure consistency,

they were made in direct comparison to complete reference specimens, and involved the use of particular shaft features where appropriate. Results for the distal humerus can be considered representative, and appear in histogram form as Figure 4.7.

For Rita-Claire and Bison Skull East, breakage points are consistent with an overall pattern of marrow cracking. The great majority of breaks occurred at or just below the level of the posterolateral foramen (d.3 and d.4), precisely where they occur in other bison and caribou-bone assemblages known or interpreted to have been heavily modified by marrow cracking (Todd and Rapson 1988: Fig. 8).

Bison Skull West presents a different picture. Only three distal humeri were recovered, but they show a fracture pattern more oriented toward the mid-shaft. Here we have to wonder what the agent of breakage was, since there was so little evidence of carnivore gnawing generally, and marrow cracking seems to be precluded by the location of the breaks. And, of course, much of the assemblage was not broken; it will be recalled that 40% of the Bison Skull West humeri were complete. The most likely process - if both carnivore action and marrow cracking are precluded - may be butchering during cold weather. Investigations by Binford (1978: 62-63) confirm that frozen carcasses are usually dismembered by breaking through longbone shafts with a hammer or axe. Unfrozen carcasses, instead, are generally disarticulated at the joints, using a small knife or even a sharp splinter of stone. At an autumn kill site like Bison Skull West, we would expect to find both complete longbones (suggestive of unfrozen butchering) and longbones broken at mid-shaft (suggestive of frozen butchering), depending on the weather and various other factors at the time of butchering.

In most precontact Inuit assemblages with which the author is familiar, disarticulation (as opposed to mid-shaft smashing) rarely leaves any preceptible traces. This seems to be a reflection of both the fragility of stone cutting

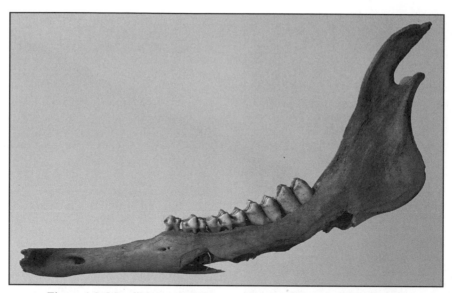

Figure 4.9. Mandible cracked for marrow extraction, Bison Skull East.

edges and the great skill employed by those doing the butchering. Fewer than two dozen specimens were noted even in the large Rita-Claire assemblage which exhibited the shallow, sharp-edged cut marks which could result from disarticulation.

Thus far we have attempted to distinguish different breaking points for upper longbones depending on whether the bone was broken by carnivores or by people engaged in marrow cracking or butchering. The situation for lower limb bones - metapodials - seems somewhat different. After all, they have a markedly different morphology and lack significant cancellous material at the articular ends. It is not surprising that they were characteristically broken in a different fashion for marrow extraction. Binford (1978: 152-153) records that the Nunamiut commonly cracked metapodials while still attached to other leg elements. The centre of the shaft was cleaned of the periosteum and then cracked with a hammer (often an articulated metacarpal and foot), resulting in a proximal metapodial still attached to the tarsals or carpals, and occasionally to the distal radial-ulna or tibia as well.

Three articulated metapodial joints were recovered from the Rita-Claire site which might reflect this pattern. One was unfortunately only described in field notes and was not collected separately, so precisely which elements were involved is unclear. The second example was collected as a unit and consisted of a complete right astragalus, a complete right calcaneus, a complete right naviculo-cuboid and a right proximal metatarsus broken in mid-shaft, all found in articulated association. In close physical association was a right proximal tibia, probably from the same animal but of course the wrong end of the bone to have been part of the same articulated bundle. The third articulated metapodial joint consisted of a distal metacarpus still in articulation with the two first phalanges (Fig. 4.8). It is likely that these articulated joints represent either the type of marrow cracking described by Binford, or frozen-carcass butchering.

Breakage Locations: Mandibles

The mandible, too, is a marrow bone, with a small marrow cavity in the corpus of the mandible directly below the cheek teeth. To reach it, it is necessary to crack open the inferior border of the mandibular corpus. There are several ways of doing so, but in

Binford's (1978: 149) Nunamiut experience the most common was to first remove the proximal and distal ends of the mandible, leaving the tooth row and adjacent corpus, which was then broken open longitudinally. A little more skill was required, but it was also possible to break open the corpus without the prior removal of the proximal and distal ends. In either case, the labour involved was great enough, and the reward small enough, that Binford's Nunamiut informants rarely bothered, citing a maxim "The wolf moves when he hears the Eskimos breaking mandibles for marrow." Binford (1978: 150) proposes that "the number of broken mandibles is a fair measure of the food security of the group in question. If many are broken, then little animal food is regularly available and the people are utilizing morsels of very limited utility."

The archaeological application of this suggestion is hampered by its taphonomic naivety; high frequencies of broken mandibles could result from any of a number of causes having nothing to do with marrow breakage. And high frequencies of broken mandibles are exactly what we encounter. At Rita-Claire the frequency of complete mandibles is just 3 out of 39, or 7.7%, and one of these, although complete as to length, has had the inferior border cracked open to expose the marrow cavity.

A more precise picture of mandibular marrow cracking can be had by looking at all mandibles with an intact tooth row. The Rita-Claire site produced nine adult examples. Of these five show longitudinal breaks exposing the marrow cavity (with or without prior removal of the proximal and distal ends) (Fig. 4.9) , while four do not. This is probably the best estimate available for Rita-Claire; slightly more than half of the mandibles (5 of 9, or 55%) were cracked for marrow. The figure from Bison Skull East is higher, although perhaps not significantly so; 4 out of 6, or 67%, while Bison Skull West again showed no evidence of mandibular marrow cracking (0 out of 2).

Bone Grease Manufacture

Gross Physical Evidence

The manufacture of bone grease consists of the heavy smashing of articular long bone ends and other elements, which are then boiled or simmered to render out the fat. The fat is skimmed off, and either stored, consumed immediately, or mixed with other foods. On the mid-continental Plains, bison bone grease was mixed with dried, pounded meat to make pemmican, a light, nutritious and easily stored food, and a crucial component of the diet for thousands of years (see Brink and Dawe 1989: 58; Reeves 1990: 170).

In the Arctic, there is little doubt that caribou bone grease was sometimes manufactured, although ethnographic descriptions are few and brief. Birket-Smith's (1929: 142-143) statement that the early 20th century Caribou Inuit boiled the fat from caribou hooves and "clean-gnawed bones" and stored the results in hide bags is typical. How the bones were boiled is left undescribed, as are the quantities involved, and the reader is left with the probably erroneous impression that the bones were boiled unbroken and intact. A slightly more specific description comes from the Copper Inuit. Here, it "sometimes happens" that all of the marrow bones — "the vertebrae, ribs, leg and feet bones" — are pounded into fragments and boiled slowly over an open fire. The rendered fat was then skimmed off and saved, "esteemed more highly perhaps than any other food the natives possess" (Jenness 1922: 103). In North Alaska, Murdoch describes the crushing of bone for two purposes; "to facilitate the trying out of the fat for making...pemmican" and to make a kind of coarse meal for dog food (Murdoch 1988: 93). The pemmican was made from "marrow" which was "extracted from reindeer bones by boiling," to which was added seal or whale blubber and boiled venison (Murdoch 1988: 63). The method of boiling is not specified, but a general description of cooking techniques suggests that, again, an open fire was normally used rather than stone boiling. In late 19th-century

Table 4.4. Derivation of a new
white grease index for caribou .

Element	Grease Value*	Volume (ml)	Grease Index	Rank
proximal humerus	40	87.0	3480	2
distal humerus	40	52.0	2080	5
prox. radioulna	48	46.0	2208	4
distal radioulna	67	21.0	1407	9
prox. metacarpus	73	8.5	621	13
distal metacarpus	78	18.5	1443	8
proximal femur	44	38.0	1672	6
distal femur	53	86.0	4558	1
proximal tibia	54	60.0	3240	3
distal tibia	73	16.0	1168	10
prox. metatarsus	71	10.0	710	12
distal metatarsus	76	19.0	1444	7
first phalanges	76	11.0	836	11
second phalanges	80	7.0	560	14
third phalanges	74	4.0	296	15

* percent fatty acids

Alaska the vessel employed would have been an iron trade pot, but Jenness's Copper Inuit were presumably using their traditional soapstone cooking pots.

Although bone grease manufacture is said to have been an ancient practise among the Copper Inuit (Jenness 1922: 103), as it probably was in Alaska as well, its status among the Mackenzie Inuvialuit is more problematic. According to Stefansson "no bones were hammered or boiled to extract the bone fat until this practice was learned from the Western Eskimo after the ships came" (Stefansson 1914: 353), a reference to the arrival of the American whaling fleet in 1889 (see Bockstoce 1986). This statement, however, should be taken as a hypothesis to be investigated rather than an absolute fact, if only because Stefansson is often an unreliable witness as to the time-depth of particular Inuvialuit customs.

On the Plains, direct physical evidence of bone grease manufacture consists of two things; boiling stones and quantities of comminuted bone. Stone boiling, however, may not have been employed in the Arctic. The few documentary sources describe open fires, and boiling stones have not been

reported from any Inuit archaeological site in Canada with which the author is familiar, although they have been identified from Palaeoeskimo contexts (Schledermann 1990). Of course, making bone grease in traditional cooking vessels of pottery or soapstone, rather than in a skin-lined pit heated with boiling stones, would drastically limit the volumes involved, since few such vessels have a capacity of more than a few litres.

Comminuted bone was encountered at the Rita-Claire site. However, as we have seen it was present in only very small quantities (total weight 135 g), and appears to represent an end product of canine digestion rather than of bone grease manufacture.

The White Grease Index

Another possible signature of bone grease manufacture would be concordance between anatomical part frequencies and a white grease index measuring potential bone grease utility. Since bone grease manufacture, unlike marrow cracking, tends to destroy or render unidentifiable the very elements being considered, the nature of the correlation might depend on how finely the bone was crushed and on the analyst's skill in making identifications from tiny fragments. Results could also depend on whether bone grease manufacture was complicated by transportation decisions, or if instead it was manufactured simply using the bones at hand. Brink and Dawe (1989: Fig. 48) report a strong negative correlation between frequency and utility from a context with abundant other evidence of bone grease manufacture at the Head-Smashed-In bison kill site.

Binford (1978) was the first to produce a white grease index, but as with his marrow index it has come under sharp criticism for involving too many variables, too many mathematical transformations, and an incorrect measure of density. As discussed by Jones and Metcalfe (1988) and Brink and Dawe (1989: 133-135), a much simpler and more accurate index can be constructed by multiplying the grease value (% fatty acids) of

Table 4.5. Spearman's rank order correlation between frequency and the grease index*

	Rita-Claire	Bison Skull East	Bison Skull West
Correlation coefficient	0.004	-0.027	0.111
Significance of correlation	>0.05	>0.05	>0.05

* juvenile elements excluded

Table 4.6. Spearman's rank order correlation between frequency and the MGUI*

	Rita-Claire	Bison Skull East	Bison Skull West
Correlation coefficient	-0.10	-0.36	-0.31
Significance of correlation	>0.05	<0.05	>0.05

* juvenile elements excluded

the part by the mean volume in millilitres of the articular end. There is no need to "norm" the results, and bone density does not appear to be a meaningful variable. Since white grease is a characteristic only of the appendicular skeleton, following Binford (1978: Table 1.12) the axial skeleton can be assigned a consistent value of 1. A new white grease index for caribou based on Binford's (1978: Table 1.11) recorded values but the simpler formula discussed above is presented in Table 4.4. Relative or ranked results are similiar but not identical to those reported by Brink and Dawe (1989: Table 20) for bison.

In keeping with the absence of gross physical evidence for bone grease manufacture, none of the three site components produced any kind of significant correlation between the new white grease index and anatomical part frequencies (MAUs) (Table 4.5). Indeed, except for Binford's (1978) Palangana site, evidence of bone grease manufacture has yet to be identified in any Arctic archaeological site, despite ethnographic evidence that it was at least an occasional activity in many areas during the early contact period.

Differential Transport and the MGUI

Another factor to be considered is meat utility. As with marrow and white grease utility, the idea — articulated by Binford (1978) and building on the work of White (e.g. 1952) and others — is a simple one: the objective "facts" of nutritional utility should (all other things being equal) underlie transportation decisions affecting the frequency of anatomical parts in faunal assemblages. Parts with a high meat utility should be associated with residential sites, while those with low utility would be discarded at kill sites. There are several indices available for measuring meat utility, including Binford's "meat utility index" and his "modified general utility index" (MGUI). This MGUI is "general" in the sense that it combines the meat, marrow, and white grease indices in a single series of values, but it is weighed so heavily in favour of the meat index that differences between it and the meat index alone are of little consequence. The MGUI is also "modified" in that values for low-utility "riders" (which might have been transported attached to larger, higher-utility parts) have been scaled up.

As with Binford's other indices, the MGUI has received some pertinent criticism. Metcalfe and Jones (1988) in particular, have noted logical inconsistencies and over-complexites in its formulation, and have suggested an alternative index which they call the food utility index, or FUI. It has not, however, come into general use, perhaps for the purely practical reason that despite its clearer and more logical formulation the FUI is essentially identical to the MGUI (see Metcalfe and Jones 1988: Fig. 3). For reasons of comparability the MGUI is retained in this study.

Spearman's Rank Order Correlations between the MGUI and assemblage MAUs are presented in Table 4.6. Once more juvenile skeletal elements were not considered when determining MAUs, since the comparability of

Table 4.7. Frequencies of burned mammal bone.

	Rita-Claire	Bison Skull East	Bison Skull West
Limited charring	n=133 (1.4%)	n=1 (0.1%)	n=1 (0.1%)
Complete charring	n=58 (0.6%)	0	0
Calcined	n=75 (0.8%)	n=1 (0.1%)	0
Total burned	n=266 (2.8%)	n=2 (0.02%)	n=1 (0.1%)

adult and juvenile element values seems questionable at best. This exclusion had little effect on the overall results, beyond a slight increase in all cases of the absolute value of rho. Correlations are consistently negative but weak; only Bison Skull East yielded a correlation with a probability of less than 0.05.

Results like these tell us essentially nothing about the role which differential transport may have played in forming the three assemblages. Negative correlations of whatever strength are characteristic of the majority of faunal assemblages, whether they represent residential sites or kill and abandonment sites (e.g. Thomas and Mayer 1983: 367-374; Le Blanc 1994: 100-108). A fairly strong "reverse utility curve," for instance, was obtained on a very large caribou sample from the residential Kugaluk site (Morrison 1988:83-90). In order to account for this unexpected result, it was suggested that Kugaluk must have functioned as a kind of provisioning or outcamp location, from which people hunted caribou for ultimate export back to a main coastal village. It is now clear (Lyman 1985, 1991; Grayson 1989) that there is a negative correlation between the MGUI and density, so that a reverse utility curve can indicate no more than density-mediated destruction, and not transport. A strong negative correlation between bone density and frequency has already been established Rita-Claire and Bison Skull East (and for that matter for Kugaluk [Morrison 1988: Fig. 25]), and is alone a probably sufficient explanation for the negative correlations obtained between frequency and the MGUI.

As a butchering site with little evidence of density-mediated destruction, it might be hoped that a clearer or more significant

negative correlation could be obtained between frequency and the MGUI at Bison Skull West. After all, the one signal success of an MGUI-based interpretative approach was at a kill and butchering site (Speth 1983), where many of the myriad factors effecting or "over-writing" assemblage composition at residential sites are not operative. However, a statistically insignificant result was obtained from Bison Skull West.

Bone Tool Manufacture

The reduction of caribou bone for purposes of tool manufacture can be easily distinguished, it is assumed, from other forms of reduction by the techniques employed. All identified examples of bone tool-making debitage demonstrated evidence of the groove-and-splinter technique as the primarily reduction strategy, in a single example only accompanied by transverse sawing. It was also limited to a single element; the metatarsal. The usual goal seems to have been the removal of the two long ridges running down the posterior face of the shaft, which in turn could be made into long, thin artifacts such as arrow heads, dart prongs, or marrow spoons (see Morrison 1986). Evidence of bone-tool manufacture was relatively sparse, but most abundant at Rita-Claire (which produced 16 worked bone specimens) and least abundant at Bison Skull West (which produced three).

A few Inuvialuit assemblages show evidence of another reduction strategy focussed on the caribou scapula, aimed at the manufacture of side-scrapers or fish scalers. A groove-and-snap technique is invariably employed in trimming the scapula to shape. No evidence of this activity was encountered at Rita-Claire or Bison Skull, although several finished (indeed broken) scapular scrapers

Table 4.8. Summary results of the analysis.

	Rita-Claire	Bison Skull East	Bison Skull West
Degree of fragmentation	most	-	least
Articular end destruction	most	-	least
Correlation with density	most	-	least
Evidence of carnivore gnawing			
—gnaw marks	most	least	-
—digested bone	most	least	-
Evidence of organic decomposition	yes	no	no
Evidence of marrow cracking	yes	yes	no
Evidence of bone grease manufacture	none	none	none
significant correlation with MGUI	none	none	none
Evidence of bone-tool manufacture	most	-	least
Evidence of burning	most	negligible	negligible

were recovered.

Instead of bone, most of the organic artifacts found at the Rita-Claire and Bison Skull sites were made of antler, and as is usual in most Inuvialuit sites essentially all of the antler recovered had been modified by groooving, chopping, and in a few cases sawing.

Burning

Burning can be a major cause of bone destruction in Inuvialuit sites, where it sometimes seems to have been used as a form of garbage disposal (Morrison 1988: 32). Burning on a large scale however was not encountered at Rita-Claire or Bison Skull. Instead, what burning is exhibited on bone specimens suggests accidental charring from cooking mishaps or the inevitable proximity of bones and open fires in a habitation area.

Three categories of burning were recognized in analysis; limited charring, complete charring, and calcination. Inevitably, the degree to which a bone specimen could be identified was conditioned by the degree of burning. Over half of the bone exhibiting limited charring could be identified to species (most of it as caribou), while few of the calcined pieces were identifiable. Some bird bone was also charred, in frequencies similar to that exhibited by the mammal bone.

As Table 4.7 illustrates, burned bone in all three categories was much more abundant at Rita-Claire than in either Bison Skull component. Since most burned bone was found in relatively close proximity to a defined hearth, this result is not surprising, since no hearths were observed at Bison Skull. The presence of burned bone in both components, albeit in tiny quantities, may suggest undiscovered hearths, although other explanations are possible. In general, though, the much greater frequency of burned bone at Rita-Claire is in keeping with other observations on the intensity of occupation at that site.

Discussion: Factors Conditioning the Composition of the Caribou Assemblages

The caribou bone assemblages have been examined in some detail, and several insights into how these assemblages were formed can or have been reached. From "architectural," locational, and other evidence the three components have already been assigned to general functional categories: Rita-Claire as an open-air camp site; Bison Skull East as a look-out/kill location, associated with hide-staking and possibly with carcass processing; and Bison Skull West as a major butchering and possible kill location. Two questions should be considered: Does the associated faunal material in any way augment or contradict these interpretations? Does it tell us anything significant we did not already know?

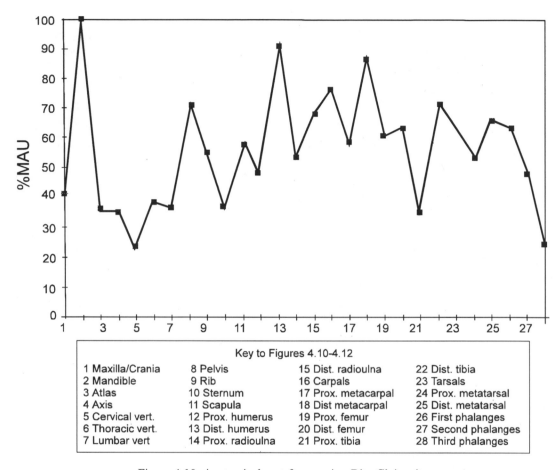

Figure 4.10. Anatomical part frequencies: Rita-Claire site.

The results of the various tests and correlations applied to the faunal assemblages in the last two chapters are summarized in Table 4.8, and can form the basis of further discussion.

Rita-Claire

As a habitation site, it is not surprising that Rita-Claire showed the strongest evidence of a variety of activities affecting the caribou bone assemblage. Included are carnivore gnawing, marrow cracking, and to a more limited extent bone-tool manufacture and burning. Coupled with relatively poor organic preservation, this has resulted in an assemblage with a very high degree of density-correlated destruction. Fragmentation is greater than in the other two assemblages, reflecting not only deliberate breakage but also the simple intensity of occupation. The relatively undifferentiated or uniform frequencies of different anatomical parts at Rita-Claire (Fig. 4.10, cf. Fig. 4.11-4.12) surely reflects, at least in part, the randomizing effect of a variety of conditioning factors.

The palimpsest effect is a major problem obscuring more detailed interpretation. From the thickness of the archaeological deposit, it must be suspected that the Rita-Claire site was occupied on a seasonal basis over a period of decades or even centuries. Inevitably, without clear stratigraphic separation the animal bones from any number of once-separate but now-indistinguishable occupations have been lumped together into a single analytical unit, blurring and averaging frequency profiles. For it cannot be considered likely that each of the occupations which contributed to our "mix" was originally identical in composition, even within the overall interpretive framework of an autumn caribou-hunting camp. Important variables conditioning what bones were brought into the site and how they were treated there would include the weather, transportation conditions, immediate nutritional or clothing needs, presence or absence of dogs, and the abundance and condition of caribou in the site catchment area, to name only a few of the more obvious factors.

The palimpsest effect is inter-occupational, and obscures by averaging or lumping. A second and probably more serious problem is operative within occupational events, and has already been referred to as "over-writing." Briefly, bones are brought into a residential site like Rita-Claire for reasons which are presumably amenable to utility-index based analysis. Once there, they are subjected to a variety of destruction forces which can obliterate the original signature. The most common destructive forces are density-mediated, and they seem to be operative in essentially all residential sites. The fact that the different utility indices are themselves correlated with density means that correlations between frequency and utility are not only obscured, they can also be misleading, as when a negative MGUI correlation is due not to differential transport but to density-mediated destruction (Lyman 1985, 1991; Grayson 1989). In most or all residential sites, it is impossible to perceive the utility-based factors which contributed to the original composition of the faunal assemblage through the subsequent over-writing of destructive, subtractive factors.

These are not the only reasons why utility indices have proved so analytically feeble. It can probably be presumed that ancient hunters did make well-informed transportation decisions based on utility. The problem lies in

the fact that utility is far too complex and ephemeral to be encapsulated in a static index. All of the caribou indices in present use are based on the nutritional facts of a single, well-nourished adult male animal, originally measured by Binford (1978). Unfortunately, depending on the condition of the animal these facts can vary enormously, and in ways for which it is practically impossible to compensate. The MGUI, for instance, is based almost entirely on the meat weight associated with a particular anatomical part (see Metcalf and Jones 1988). For most of the year, however, the nutritional utility of different cuts of caribou is based not on meat weight, but fat content. Observations made by the wildlife biologist A.H. Lawrie in the 1940's (quoted in Kelsall 1968: 209-211) are worth repeating at length:

> An entirely protein diet is nutritionally inadequate. This the eskimo [*sic*] recognizes and the rule of a mouthful of fat for a mouthful of lean meat prevails.... This need for fat while on a meat diet imposes apparently wasteful habits on the eskimo. Thus in the late spring and summer caribou have little fat save in the tongue and marrow while its progressive deposition [elsewhere]... occurs in the fall. In the late spring and summer eskimo were repeatedly observed to take only the tongue and the lower part of the limbs from their kills - the lean meat, unfortified with fat, being untouched. As the fall progressed the choice of cuts constantly widened until every part of the caribou was utilized save the viscera, neck, shoulders, and thighs which were fed to the dogs.

The important point is not merely that utility varies with nutritional state, but rather that it does not vary uniformly from element to element. Different elements might have relatively low utility values in one season of the year, and relatively high values at another, while their index values remain static. Lower limb elements, for instance, have a low MGUI

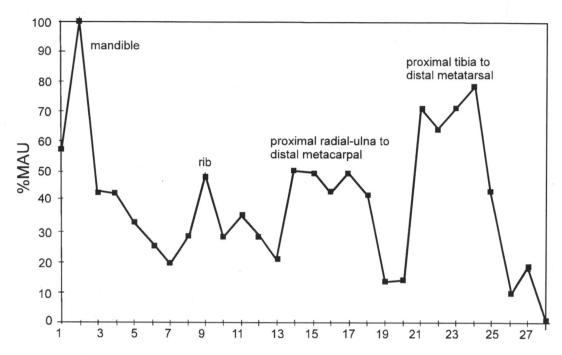

Figure 4.11. Anatomical part frequencies: Bison Skull East (see Fig. 4.10 for key).

value but a high marrow index, while mandibles (in association with tongues) are low in both (see Binford 1978: Table 2.7; and Table 4.3, above). A faunal assemblage dominated by metapodials and mandibles would make no sense at all in terms of any current utility index, yet made perfect nutritional sense to the Inuit hunters observed by Lawrie. The fact that relative utility can also vary markedly by sex and age (see Stefansson 1946, 1962, *passim*) only further complicates the matter, particularly since age and sex can be only very imperfectly controlled for in an archaeological caribou assemblage (see below). The real world is harder to model than we might hope.

Bison Skull East

Many of these same problems are illustrated in the Bison Skull East assemblage. Here fragmentation values were again relatively high, suggesting the fairly intensive use both of the component area and of the caribou bones brought into it. Carnivore gnawing, however, was very poorly

represented, with few obvious gnaw marks and no evidence of digested bone, an observation in keeping with the inferred function of the component. Dogs would be expected at a residential site like Rita-Claire, presumably tethered and deliberately fed, with small concentrations of comminuted fecal bone suggesting a dog yard. But it is very difficult to imagine that people would tolerate the presence of dogs at a lookout and kill site, where their barking and general clamour could only spoil the hunting. What little evidence of gnawing there is can probably be attributed to the scavenging of wolves after its human occupants had left.

Marrow cracking is the one activity which seems to be well represented at the Bison Skull East, although by breakage patterns only. Neither it nor any other activity seems to be clearly reflected in utility/frequency correlations. This does not mean, however, that the frequency profile from Bison Skull East (Fig. 4.11) is an amorphous jumble. Instead, it bears a striking resemblance to the kind of utility pattern described by Lawrie, above. Mandible and mid- and lower limb element frequencies are high, along with only one other element; namely ribs. Does this mean that Bison Skull East was occupied in the spring or early summer, that the caribou they were processing were in poor nutritional shape and people were exploiting mainly marrow bones and tongues?

Cautiously, we may answer no. For one thing, the seasonal evidence already examined clearly indicates that the caribou fauna at Bison Skull East represents an autumn kill, the one season of the year when caribou generally, and bulls in particular, are in prime nutritional shape. Moreover, Bison Skull East is a kill/lookout location and not a residential site. It would not be expected that the caribou bone found there would represent the high-utility products of primary butchering, but rather food in the form of snacks or simple meals brought in from elsewhere, to be eaten while watching or waiting for game. If field butchering were undertaken on animals killed in the immediate vicinity of the shooting blinds, we could also expect to find low-utility parts which had been abandoned after butchering, along with parts of various utility which had been consumed on the spot.

Binford (1978) spent considerable time studying faunal assemblages associated with ethnographic Nunamiut autumn hunting stands in northern Alaska. One clear conclusion was the great importance of marrow bones in the "snacking" diet of waiting hunters. Indeed, "All hunting stands exhibited a form modeled by criteria of marrow-bone selection.... The assemblages were variable, primarily depending on the character of the population from which the choice of marrow bones was made and whether provisions were introduced to the location from the residential sites" (Binford 1978: 484). In all of the stands, the most frequent parts were those of the mid- to lower rear leg (i.e. tibia, tarsals, and metatarsals), while frequencies of mandibles (also a marrow bone) and front legs were more variable, depending on the factors noted above. Vertebrae, scapula, and pelvis frequencies are consistently low (Binford

1978: 359). These relative frequencies find some basis in the marrow utility index, but could not be predicted directly from it.

The fit between expectations (as represented by ethnoarchaeological hunting stands) and reality at Bison Skull East is relatively close, even if it is *post hoc*. After mandibles, the highest frequencies are on the mid- to lower rear leg, while mid to lower front leg frequencies are also high. The Big and Little Happy Valley stands studied by Binford (1978: Fig. 7.14) produced particularly similar frequency profiles, including even the very high mandible spike and a more minor frequency rise for ribs. Tentatively, it is concluded that the caribou assemblage from Bison Skull East has been strongly (but probably not exclusively) conditioned by marrow bone selection, and that this in turn is strongly related to its function as a hunting stand or lookout/kill site. Whether the Nunamiut devotion to marrow-bone snacking at such sites is "culturally" or "economically" based can remain unresolved, given the very close cultural relationship and common cultural origin shared by Alaskan Nunamiut and Mackenzie Inuvialuit.

If the above arguments are accepted, we can wonder why the Spearman's Rank Order correlation between frequency and the marrow index at this site was not stronger (rho=0.22, p>0.05). One likely answer is that a rank order correlation may not always be the best device for comparing the fit between frequency and utility. Because it ignores amplitude, the difference between a %MAU of 25.6 and one of 25.7, for instance, is given the same weight as the difference between a %MAUs of 25.7 and one of 90.0, as long as the rank order change is constant. A rank order correlation is thus easily confused by "noise" in the form of relatively minor and essentially meaningless frequency fluctuations, while the kind of large-scale frequency changes that may be the real signatures of the assemblage can be essentially invisible. In the case of Bison Skull East, the visual inspection of the frequency profile reveals major patterns which are missed in an element-by-element rank order correlation.

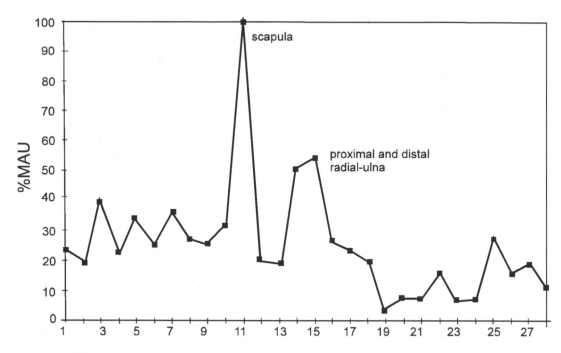

Figure 4.12. Anatomical part frequencies: Bison Skull West (see Fig. 4.10 for key).

The poor fit between frequency and marrow utility may also reflect, once again, the simplistic and static nature of any utility index, or at least the uses to which it is standardly put. As Binford points out, marrow bone selection at a hunting stand depends not only on utility but also availability, in this case "the character of the population from which the choice of marrow bones was made and whether provisions were introduced to the location from the residential sites" (Binford 1978: 484). In an ethnoarchaeological study, Binford is able to directly investigate availability (see Binford 1978: Table 7.5) and model its effects on marrow bone selection (see Binford 1978: Tables 7.8 and 7.9). We, investigating the mute past, cannot so easily do so.

Bison Skull West

To a large extent, the Rita-Claire and Bison Skull site assemblages can be seen as three distinct points along the same continuum of variability, with Rita-Claire occupying one end of the range and Bison Skull West the

other. It shows the least evidence of fragmentation, the least evidence of marrow cracking, the least evidence of density-mediated destruction, and the least evidence of burning and of bone-tool manufacture. Bone breakage at the site may have been partially conditioned by cold-weather butchering, as reflected in the mid-shaft smashing of longbones, but few other causative agents or processes could be identified. In general, the Bison Skull West assemblage seems to have been the least heavily utilized or modified of the three, an observation which is certainly in keeping with a suggested function as a primary butchering location. There is no evidence of the kind of intensive bone processing which sometimes accompanies butchering in some Plains bison-kill sites (e.g. Brink and Dawe 1989).

Overall anatomical-part frequencies from Bison Skull West are similarly the least like those from Rita-Claire (Fig. 4.12). The Rita-Claire profile is relatively undifferentiated, with most elements (except for vertebrae and the proximal tibia) achieving %MAUs above

50. It has been suggested that this reflects the averaging effects of a complex history of site use, where the assemblage has been conditioned by a large number of different additive and subtractive factors. The Bison Skull West profile, by contrast, is dominated by only a very few elements — notably the scapula and a much lesser extent the proximal and distal radio-ulna — so much so that no other element achieves a %MAU greater than 40.

It is suspected that this high degree of *differentiation* within the Bison Skull West assemblage reflects an overall component assemblage which is both highly structured spatially, and inadequately sampled archaeologically. The discovery in a single one-metre square of 25 scapula, most of them complete, suggests the kind of single-element groupings seen in structured butchering sites elsewhere (e.g. Wheat 1972). Having suffered so little from density-mediated and other forms of bone destruction, it could be hoped that a larger, more representative sample might be very informative of the kinds of elements abandoned at an autumn butchering location. However, if the assemblage is as large, dense, and spatially structured as it seems to be, a representative sample might have to be very large indeed.

Part III: Special Cases

In this section we investigate several of Binford's (1978) "special cases"; particular elements where distinctive breakage or butchering patterns have been suggested to be unusually revealing of past economic activities. We will also review the skeletal representation of juvenile caribou, to determine if the contrast with mature skeletal representation reveals anything about the specific uses to which calves-of-the-year might have been put. Again the primary goal is to generate or validate observations which might be helpful in the analysis of caribou and other ungulate faunal assemblages. As in previous sections, specific results are rarely definitive, but it may be hoped that a growing body of comparative data might still lead to insights into the very complex processes that condition the composition of faunal asemblages.

Ribs

Ribs are among the few elements which can be successfully dried with the bone in, as well as frozen or consumed fresh. In his study of Nunamiut caribou consumption patterns, Binford (1978: 151-152) noted that fresh boiled or roasted ribs were usually broken into "rib tablets" one to four inches in length (3-10 cm) on consumption, so that the "blood marrow" inside could be either sucked out or could contribute to the stew. In the case of dried or frozen ribs this blood marrow was usually rancid or at least sour tasting, so that dried or frozen ribs were invariably left unbroken. Binford (1978: 152) proposed that high ratios of broken ribs in an archaeological context should be a "fairly direct monitor of the amount of fresh meat being consumed," while "low ratios should reflect consumption of dried or frozen stores."

This suggestion, like several others by Binford, is rather naive from a taphonomic point of view. Considering all the agents and processes which could possibly break ribs in both an occupational and, later, in a depositional context, it would seem foolhardy in the extreme to suggest that any particular set of ribs had been broken specifically for consumption in the form of rib tablets. However, the obverse face of the suggestion may have some merit. Broken ribs tell us nothing, but relatively high ratios of complete ribs should indeed — if Binford's observations can be generalized — indicate the consumption of dried or frozen stores. We should certainly not expect high ratios of complete ribs in any of our three Cape Bathurst assemblages, particularly at a habitation site like Rita-Claire. As have seen, this site gives every indication of having been occupied during the autumn by people who were actively engaged in caribou hunting; people who probably had as much fresh meat as they could eat and who certainly were not living off dried or frozen stores.

Figure 4.13. Caribou heads on a modern meat rack.

The relevant calculation would be the ratio of complete ribs over the total rib MNE (based on a count of proximal ends). For the Rita-Claire site this figure is 111/285 or 39%. It would be higher if nearly complete ribs were also included, and over 75% if it included all rib portions more than 10 cm long. Percent complete figures for Bison Skull East and West are 53% and 55% respectively.

Of course, without direct comparisons it is difficult to determine whether these are "high" ratios, but they certainly *seem* high, especially considering the degree of fragmentation exhibited by the assemblages in general. Tentatively, Binford's proposal does not seem promising, and it may be that the failure to break ribs into tablets was conditioned by more than just the condition of the "blood marrow." Additional data from other sites would be useful.

Crania

Binford's (1978: 150-151) Nunamiut treated caribou heads in different ways depending on how they were to be used. During the early half of the autumn hunt, when hides were prime for clothing, it was usual to skin the heads in such as way that they could be easily fashioned into parka hoods. This meant that the antlers had to be removed before skinning (except in the case of the very youngest animals) and the skin then cut away from around the antler bases, so that the skin of the head was removed intact. "Typically," Binford suggests, "animals skinned for clothing materials have chopped-off antlers and circular cuts around the antler bases."

This skinning strategy, of course, would apply only to groups who made parka hoods out of head skins, or had some other need to remove the head skin as a unit, something

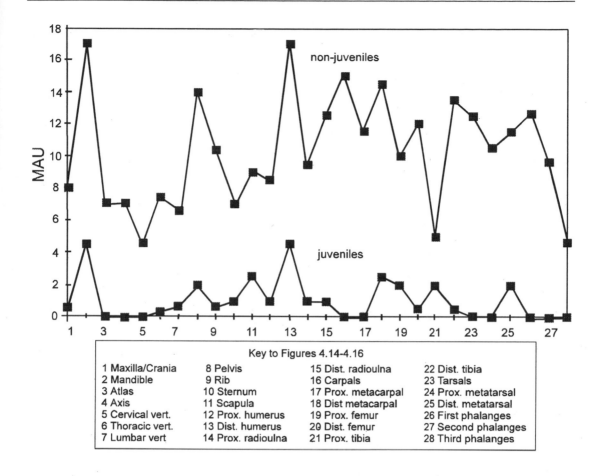

Figure 4.14. Juvenile and non-juvenile caribou: Rita-Claire.

which can hardly be assumed for all arctic cultures using caribou skin for clothing. However it is not unreasonable to suggest that it may apply to the Inuvialuit and most other Inuit, who did, in fact, normally cut their parka hoods from caribou heads, with the ears on. Our evidence for this is ethnographic, but it is so widespread a pattern that it is probably ancient, and of considerable symbolic importance (Savoie 1970: 171; see also Jenness 1946: 12; Hall et al. 1994: 19, 28-29).

An alternative strategy was employed when heads were intended solely for food. Skinning was a much less elaborate affair, with longitudinally-oriented cut marks between the antlers and eyes. If boiling was intended, after skinning the heads were generally split longitudinally, opening the brain case and exposing the fat in the nose and behind the eyes (Jenness [1922: 103] indicates that the Copper Inuit quartered their heads). The antlers were sometimes left attached to serve as handles, particularly if roasting was intended, but they were generally removed in the case of heads which were to be boiled in a small pot. Juvenile, immature, and to a lesser extent young-adult female heads were preferred over those from adult males for eating (see also Kelsall 1968: Tables 26 and 27, for data on a similar Canadian Inuit preference).

Rita-Claire produced only seven cranial

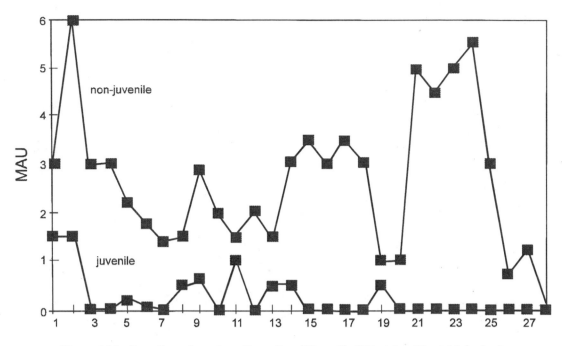

Figure 4.15. Juvenile and non-juvenile caribou: Bison Skull East (see Fig. 4.14 for key).

(frontal) portions large enough to include antler bases. Three specimens consist of both the right and left-sided portion, undivided. The other specimens consist of 2 rights and 2 lefts, separated at or near the medial suture. Both rights are nearly complete cranial halves, including not only the frontal but also the parietal, temporal, and a portion of the occipital bones. Medial edges are not well enough preserved to absolutely confirm purposeful cutting or chopping, but its seems very likely that these two specimens (and possibly the two lefts as well) were deliberately opened for cooking and eating.

No specimen exhibited any significant portion of attached antler; most had clearly been removed by breaking or cutting. Only one showed any skinning or cut marks; one of the "opened" cranial specimen described above, which has a single, short, sharp nick at the antler base, possibly indicative of skinning around the antler. Another specimen with an intact but eroded antler bud was of a size suggesting a juvenile animal of about three to

five months of age, while at least two others seem to represent either females or immature male (1-2 years old) animals. None of the specimens could be clearly identified as an adult male on the basis of antler-base morphology (see Speiss 1979: 97-100).

Bison Skull East produced three frontal elements with attached antler bases. There are two lefts and a right, all of a size suggesting animals in the three to five months age cohort. The antlers consist of mere buds; two of them are intact and one has been sliced off, seemingly with a sharp knife. No other cut marks were visible, nor was there any evidence of the deliberate splitting of skulls.

Bison Skull West produced only a single frontal fragment with an attached antler base. It too was from a juvenile animal about three to five months in age, with an intact antler bud. It is a right frontal element, and again exhibits no skinning or other cut marks.

With only a single visible skinning mark, it

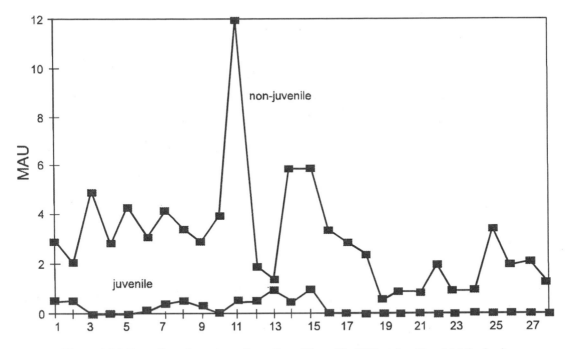

Figure 4.16. Juvenile and non-juvenile caribou: Bison Skull West (see Fig. 4.14 for key).

remains unresolved whether any of these Bison Skull and Rita-Claire cranial fragments or the animals they represent were skinned for clothing purposes. Evidence of splitting - and hence of cooking and eating - seems clearer, although at least three crania from Rita-Claire had clearly not been split. Unfortunately, the relative frequency of split crania is obscured by the many juvenile specimens. With their open medial sutures, juvenile frontals are not likely to yield evidence of mid-line chopping or cutting, and in any event will naturally separate in the course of organic decomposition.

The high proportion of juvenile crania, particularly at Bison Skull, may reflect the uses to which heads were put. It certainly agrees with traditional Inuit taste, which much favours younger and/or female over adult male heads for consumption. However, how this relates to site function remains puzzling. The juvenile cranium found at Bison Skull West, for instance, presumably represents discard without consumption, given the function of

that site area, while the crania from Bison Skull East might as well, unless they represent "snack food" brought in from elsewhere. The bias in favour of juvenile heads is weakest at Rita-Claire, the one location where, as a habitation site, heads are most likely to have been cooked and consumed.

Juvenile Representation

As the above discussion demonstrates, there are clear differences in the representation of skeletal elements between adult and younger animals. It will be recalled that juvenile elements were explicitly not considered in most of the anatomical-part studies presented in earlier chapters, since they differ so markedly from their adult counterparts, particularly with regard to density. We will now compare adult and juvenile representation, in order to see what kinds of patterned differences there are. Tentative interpretations may be occasionally offered, but for the most part the goal is simply descriptive. Considering the importance

Table 4.9. Percent complete:
juvenile vs. non-juvenile elements.

Element	% complete juvenile	% complete non-juvenile
Rita-Claire		
mandible	20.0	5.9
ribs	35.3	39.0
scapula	60.0	38.9
radius	50.0	0.0
Bison Skull East		
mandible	50.0	25.0
ribs	37.5	45.3
scapula	100.0	66.7
Bison Skull West		
mandible	100.0	25.0
ribs	55.5	53.2
scapula	100.0	91.7
humerus	50.0	25.0
radius	50.0	41.7

of density as the major factor conditioning anatomical-part frequencies in most archaeological assemblages — including the ones studied here — it is difficult to proceed much further, until more is known of juvenile representation in other assemblages, and until density studies based specifically on juvenile elements are available.

The contrast is between the very youngest animals in our three assemblages — juveniles, aged three to five months — and all other animals, the next youngest of which are about a year older. In so doing we are doubtlessly blurring distinctions between immature animals fifteen to seventeen months old and those a year or more older still, but the nature of the data make it difficult to further subdivide the age categories. Immatures of fifteen to seventeen months are approaching adult size, and some of their longbone epiphyses have fused (see Speiss 1979: Table 3:15). In short, they cannot always be distinguished from adults. This is not the case with three-to-five-month juveniles, whose live weight at about 15 kg is about one-seventh that of an adult animal.

Juvenile elements were identified with reference to a one-to-two-month old (late July) wolf-kill specimen in the

zooarchaeological collections of the Canadian Museum of Civilization (catalogue number F-1137-5). Archaeological specimens were found to be consistently larger than this individual by an estimated 10 to 20 percent, while a three-to-five-month age estimate is confirmed by dental eruption patterns (see chapters 3 and 5). Juvenile and non-juvenile anatomical-part frequencies for the three component assemblages are presented in Figures 4.14-4.16. In order to graph differences in the absolute magnitude of representation, frequencies are presented as MAUs rather than %MAUs.

This is the first study to contrast juvenile and non-juvenile caribou anatomical part frequencies from an archaeological or any other context. In the absence of comparative information only a few obvious observations can be made. In all three assemblages, juvenile and non-juvenile element frequencies form two non-overlapping distribution curves, with the non-juvenile curve being higher than the juvenile curve by a whole order of magnitude. To use Rita-Claire as an example, the *average* MAU for the 28 elements considered is 10.3 for non-juveniles and 1.0 for juveniles.

Spearman's Rank Order Correlations are uniformly insignificant (p>0.05) when comparing juvenile-element frequencies with general utility (MGUI), density (as determined for adults), or non-juvenile frequencies. In part this is certainly due to the large number of ties in the juvenile data set, a fact that reflects the low absolute numbers involved. Using Rita-Claire as an example again, out of a total of 28 elements there is one 10-way tie in MAUs, two 4-way ties, one 3-way tie, and two 2-way ties. Under such situations meaningful correlation will rarely if ever be demonstrable (see Siegel 1956: 207-210).

Looking beyond rank order correlations, a few general patterns do seem apparent. At Rita-Claire, where juvenile figures are absolutely higher than in the other two assemblages, there is some apparent overall agreement between juvenile and non-juvenile anatomical-part representation, with many of

Figure 4.17. By autumn, caribou calves can easily outrun any predator.

the "spikes" in the non-juvenile MAUs reflected in the juvenile MAUs (mandible, pelvis, distal humerus). This does not seem to be the case with the two Bison Skull components. The importance of limb or marrow bones in the Bison Skull East assemblage has no reflection in the juvenile elements, nor does the high frequency of scapulae at Bison Skull West. In both of these assemblages the juvenile appendicular skeleton is very poorly represented.

A more clear-cut difference between juvenile and non-juvenile caribou bone in the Rita-Claire and Bison Skull assemblages is the relative frequency of complete bones (%complete). Juvenile bone is much less dense than the bone of older animals (Munson 1991), and should survive complete (or at all) much less often. Yet %complete figures for juvenile elements are generally higher than for non-juveniles. Only certain elements can be compared; the vertebrae and innominate, for instance, have not yet fused together in the case of juveniles and hence cannot be complete. Elements which are not represented in the juvenile sample or where both

%complete scores were 0 must also be excluded. Percent complete scores for the remaining elements are presented in Table 4.9.

It seems that juvenile skeletal elements are less subject to breakage than non-juvenile elements. This appears to be especially true of the mandible, radius, and humerus - all of them marrow bones. Indeed the rarity with which juvenile marrow bones were cracked suggests that they were rarely exploited for their marrow. This is a rather puzzling observation, since juvenile longbones have smaller volumes but are otherwise as rich in marrow fats as their adult counterparts (Davis et al. 1987: 367). Their marrow cavities, in fact, are larger than those of adult mandibles, yet they appear to have been much more rarely broken to extract marrow (or for any other purpose). It may be, that except possibly for their heads and tongues, caribou calves were rarely considered a food item by the site's inhabitants, a situation for which there are good ethnographic parallels in the Central Arctic (see Kelsall 1968: Tables 26 and 27). Whether or not this is an example of economic behaviour remains unclear.

Chapter 5

The Age and Sex of the Caribou

Introduction

It has become common practise in many areas to determine the age and sex profiles of herd-animal dominated faunal assemblages in order to understand better the decision-making processes of ancient hunters. As a result, excellent osteometric data are now available for assessing age and sex in a number of important species (e.g. Reher and Frison 1980; Klein et al. 1981; Klein and Cruz-Uribe 1984; Todd 1987). Caribou, however, have proved difficult to deal with, for several reasons. They are less sexually dimorphic than many ungulate species, particularly bison, so that few discrete measurements are capable of distinguishing adult males from females with acceptable accuracy (Miller 1974). As well, caribou teeth are lower crowned than those of most other ungulates, so that attrition from wear over a given period of time is less. It has thus proved impossible to group caribou mandibles-with-teeth into seasonal cohorts on the basis of metaconid heights, as is commonly possible with bison at kill sites (e.g. Reher 1974). Instead, the few studies which have attempted to look at caribou age structure have been based on gross tooth wear and eruption categories (Speiss 1979; Gronnow et al. 1983), or destructive and expensive dental thin-sectioning (Miller 1974).

In this chapter we examine the age and sex structure of the Bison Skull and Rita-Claire caribou assemblages.

Age

The most reliable techniques for estimating the age-at-death of caribou are based on mandibles and the teeth within them.

In the case of immature animals, age can be estimated from dental eruption patterns, which are well known for caribou and precise enough to be appropriate (Miller 1974). In the case of dentally mature animals, age can estimated from the buccal crown height of the first molar (m1) (Fig. 5.1). A sample of 78 barrenground caribou mandibles of known age were measured for this feature (Morrison and Whitridge 1997). A strong linear regression was found to exist between crown height and age, expressed in the formula:

age (in months) = -12.56 * crown height (in mm) + 186.97

In species with more high-crowned molars than caribou, the relationship between age and crown height has been found - or assumed - to be a slightly curvilinear one, requiring a geometric or even cubic solution, rather than the arithmetic, straight-line solution proposed above (see Klein et al. 1981, 1983). Because caribou have relatively low-crowned teeth, absolute attrition over time is so slight that a curvilinear relationship, if present at all, seems to be unmeasureable. Test results indicate that the formula presented above is accurate to within about a year. Both measuring accuracy and individual variation are likely to be implicated in this error factor, which is too great to justify the use of crown height for seasonal determinations.

The first step in estimating ages is to sort the mandibles from each site or component into independent samples. At minimum these could consist of all the left mandibles, or all the right mandibles, from a given component. In order to maximize sample size, however, it was considered feasible to include any opposite-side specimens which were clearly

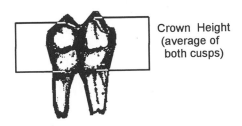

Crown Height
(average of
both cusps)

Figure 5.1. Measuring the crown height of m1.

Table 5.1. Mandibles by age .

Catalogue number	Eruption category	Crown height	Side	Age in years
Rita-Claire				
210c	m1 erupting	-	r	<1
186a	m1 erupting	-	r	<1
206b	m1 erupting	-	r	<1
588	m1 erupting	-	r	<1
186c	m1 erupting	-	r	<1
577b	m2 erupted	-	r	1
611a	m2 erupted	-	r	1
210d	m3 erupting	-	r	1
577a	m3 erupting	-	r	1
198a	dentally mature	12.8	l	2
210a	dentally mature	12.7	r	2
592	dentally mature	9.5	l	5
611b	dentally mature	8.8	r	6
198b	dentally mature	8.0	r	7
210e	dentally mature	7.5	r	7
580a	dentally mature	4.5	l	10
186d	dentally mature	3.7	r	11
Bison Skull East				
148d	m1 erupting	-	l	<1
140	m1 erupting	-	l	<1
144b	m2 erupted	-	l	1
148c	m3 erupting	-	r	1
144c	dentally mature	12.4	r	2
144a	dentally mature	11.7	l	3
140	dentally mature	8.9	l	6
151	dentally mature	6.75	l	8
148b	dentally mature	-	r	10+
Bison Skull West				
153d	m1 erupting	-	l	<1
153c	dentally mature	12.0	r	3
153a	dentally mature	9.7	r	5
153b	dentally mature	8.9	r	6

unpaired; i.e. the sample might consist of all the left mandibles from a given component, along with any right mandibles which from metric or other observations could not possibly be paired with any of the lefts. The intention is to ensure that each specimen in the sample uniquely represents a single animal. Ages in months or years can then be calculated as appropriate.

Eruption categories and m1 crown heights for mandibles from our three assemblages are presented in Table 5.1. The resulting age profiles are presented as Figures 5.2-5.4.

Interpreting these or any other age profiles is more difficult than producing them, and much more problematic than is usually assumed (see for example Speiss 1979, Gronnow et al 1983). Several potentially major problems can be discussed, each with possibly profound implications concerning the reliability of samples, and particularly the comparability of adult vs. immature age frequencies.

Identification Problems

Because different criteria were used in estimating the ages of adult and immature animals, they are differentially identifiable. Specimens identified by immature eruption are immediately assignable to a one-year age range: animals with m1 erupting are less than one-year old, while animals with m3 erupting and/or m2 erupted are one year old (actually 12-27 months). This is not true of dentally mature specimens, which require, at minimum, an intact and measureable m1. Moreover, and more seriously, mandibles from animals under one year of age are much more likely than others to be complete (see chapter 6), and can be identified on the basis of size and texture alone, while older animals cannot be so distinguished. The effect is to underestimate the number of adults when constructing age histograms.

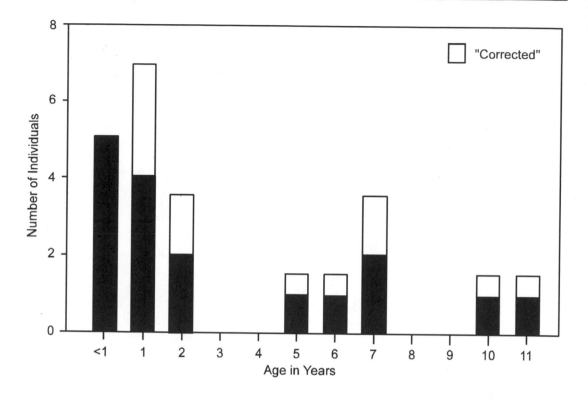

Figure 5.2. Age structure of the Rita-Claire site caribou.

This problem can be quite a serious one. At Rita-Claire, the MNI on mandibles was 26, counting at the left mental foramen. Yet because of the fragmentary nature of the assemblage, not all of these 26 can easily be accounted for. The MNI on specimens intact enough through the molar row to be placed in one of our three eruption categories is only 17; the less-than-one-year age category has an MNI of 5, the 1-year old category has an MNI of 4, and the adult or dentally mature category has an MNI of 8. This leaves a minimum of 9 individuals unaccounted for, represented by isolated medial portions with the mental foramen and in some cases associated premolars. From their size, texture, and the fact that all of the extant premolars are permanent, none could be juvenile, but it is not certain that all are adults. Even if we assume they are adults, none includes the m1 necessary for a precise age estimate. In short, we have precise age estimates for all five

juvenile animals represented in the Rita-Claire assemblage, but only 12 out of 21 non-juvenile animals.

Because of small and less fragmented mandible assemblages the situation was less problematic at the two Bison Skull components. At Bison Skull West a mandibular MNI of four was equal to the number of readable independent samples. At Bison Skull East the mandibular MNI of nine included two juveniles, two immatures, and five adults. One of these adult specimens was missing the m1, but an age estimate of 10+ could still be made based on gross wear on the other cheek teeth.

It is difficult to suggest how this problem of unequal identification could be addressed. It might be assumed that the non-juvenile mandibles for which we can estimate a precise age are representative of the total population

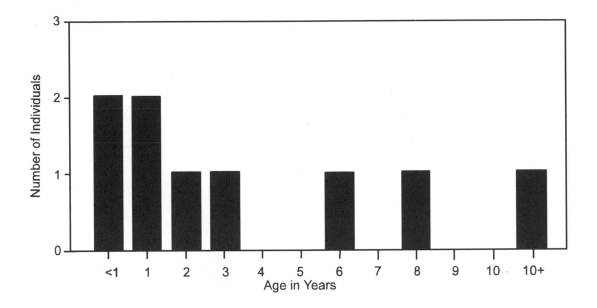

Figure 5.3. Age structure of the Bison Skull East caribou.

from which they were derived. In other words, it could be proposed that of the nine unaccounted-for MNIs at Rita-Claire, three are 1-year olds and six are adults, preserving the 2:1 ratio of adults over 1-year olds seen in the accounted-for portion of the sample. The frequency values in each adult 1-year age category could then be multiplied by 1.75 ((8+6)/8) to account for the addition of the 6 additional adults. This was the solution proposed by Morrison and Whitridge (1997) in attempting to establish age profiles for caribou at two other Inuvialuit archaeological sites in the western Arctic, and as one way of dealing with the situation it is reflected in the "corrected" age profile seen on the Rita-Claire histogram (Fig. 5.2). But it seems a not-entirely satisfactory way out of our difficulties, particularly in light of the second potential problem, for which even an arbitrary solution seems elusive. For if identification problems tend toward the overestimation of adults, the problem of differential survivorship tends in the opposite direction.

Survivorship

Immature skeletal elements, including mandibles, are less dense and hence more vulnerable to destruction than their adult counterparts. In a review of white-tailed deer mortality profiles from the eastern United States, Munson (1991) notes that many archaeological assemblages have been interpreted as indicated a hunting bias in favour of prime-age adults, when most or all of the discrepency can instead be attrituted to the much greater survivability of mature over immature elements. In a heavily gnawed sheep assemblage, he found that only 6% of mandibles in the less-than-one-year age category survived, as compared to 50% of 1-year olds, 80% of 2-year olds, and 88% of 5-year olds. We already know that the Rita-Claire or Bison Skull East caribou assemblages have been seriously ravaged, and we must expect that the frequency of younger individuals represented in both samples has been greatly reduced.

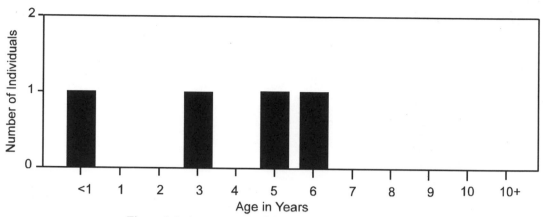

Figure 5.4. Age structure of the Bison Skull West caribou.

Unfortunately it seems impossible to determine how greatly they have been reduced. In constructing age histograms, should we multiply mandible frequencies by correction factors of 14.7 for less-than-one-year-olds (88/6) and 1.8 for 1-year olds (88/50)? Probably not. Juvenile mandibles are already the most abundant one-year age category in all three assemblages; multiplied by a factor of almost fifteen they would dominate the age profiles to an extent that is simply not believable. Juvenile and indeed all immature mandibles are almost certainly under-represented because of density-mediated destruction, but the degree to which this is true remains unknown, and probably unknowable.

Transportation

As was discussed in Chapter 4, Inuit (and probably most other caribou-hunting people) prefer to eat the heads of younger caribou, often abandoning the heads of older animals at kill locations. Mandibles often "ride" with these heads, so that, as Binford (1978: 150-151) warns, an age profile based on mandibles can be heavily and quite incorrectly skewed in favour of younger animals. He cites as an example a recent Nunamiut camp whose inhabitants reported a heavy hunting bias in favour of adult male caribou, but where the cranial evidence in the middens (and presumably the mandibular evidence as well)

suggested that over 90% of animals killed were females or yearlings.

Unlike the problems of survivorship and identification, differential transport based on age seems not to have been operative in the assemblages under investigation. At both Rita-Claire and Bison Skull East, adult (or at least non-juvenile) caribou mandibles have a %MAU of 100, and are clearly not under-represented in relation to other skeletal elements. This is also true of juveniles, indicating that mandibles are consistently the most abundant element regardless of age. As we saw in Chapter 4, there is evidence that cranium representation had been biased in favour of younger and/female animals. Since this does not seem to be the case with mandibles it is likely that they were transported independently of crania, probably in assocation with tongues.

Although results were negative at Rita-Claire and Bison Skull East, in other situations where the mandibular %MAU is significantly higher for juvenile than for non-juvenile caribou, differential transport of the sort described by Binford should be suspected.

Interpretation

The interpretation of age profiles is based on a comparison between the overall shape of the histogram and a number of ideal patterns,

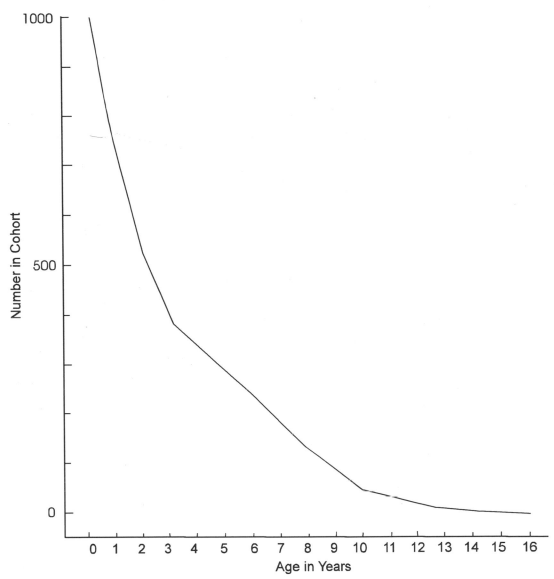

Figure 5.5. Age structure of the Kaminuriak caribou herd. (after Miller 1974: Fig. 22)

including a *catastrophic* or *L-shaped* curve, where the archaeological age profile resembles that of the natural population from which it was derived; an *attritional* or *U-shaped* curve, where the very young and old are represented to the near exclusion of prime-age adults, and its inverse, an *n-shaped* curve where prime-age adults dominate (Klein and Cruz-Uribe 1984: 57-99; Stiner 1991). A catastrophic age profile should reflect communal, mass-slaughter hunting, where little or no discrimination on the part of the hunters is possible. An n-shaped curve reflects the deliberate targetting of prime-age adults (taphonomic factors being equal), which in the case of caribou is usually the most desirable age group (best nutritional condition) but also the fleetest and hardest to kill. Finally, a U-shaped curve reflects the selective or encounter hunting of the weakest and most vulnerable but not generally the most valuable age groups.

Estimating the age structure of the natural population from which our kill populations were derived is based on assumptions. The size of barrenground caribou herds can fluctuate enormously, depending on various poorly-understood factors including hunting pressure, weather, and range destruction from fire or other causes (Kelsall 1968). All will have an effect on the age structure of a herd; heavy hunting pressure, for instance, may increase the relative proportion of younger animals, while sleet on the calving grounds may decrease it. None of these factors can be controlled for when dealing with the Bluenose caribou herd of 300 or 400 years ago. The best available information takes the form of a snap-shot picture of the age structure of the Kaminuriak barrenground herd over a several-year period in the 1960s (Fig. 5.5). It is very heavily dominated by animals in the first three or four years of life, with a very steep mortality curve. It is presumed that the age structure of animals available to the inhabitants of the Rita-Claire and Bison Skull sites was not greatly dissimilar.

None of the archaeological age profiles is based on a large enough sample to present a smooth curve. That from Bison Skull West is, in fact, too small to be "read" at all. The profiles from Bison Skull East and Rita-Claire, on the other hand, seem similar to one another, regardless of whether the "corrected" or uncorrected Rita-Claire scores are used. Both could probably be best categorized as "modified catastrophic"; that is they show a trend toward decreasing frequency with age, but the slope is much less steep than the natural population profile, and relatively flat through the adult portion. As discussed, some of this comparative gentleness of slope may be due to differential taphonomic destruction in the youngest age categories. It may also imply a degree of selectivity, however minor, on the

part of Rita-Claire and Bison Skull site hunters, favouring the capture of older, larger, and fatter animals within a generally catastrophic kill environment (cf. Gronnow et al. 1983: 74-75).

Detailed age estimates are available from three other western Arctic caribou assemblages (Morrison and Whitridge 1997). Two, dating to the mid-19th century, have profiles which are very similar to those from Rita-Claire and Bison Skull, while the third - dating to the late 19th century - presented a classic n-shaped profile. It seems likely that the introduction of firearms in the 1870s is the major factor responsible for the change, which implies a shift from communal hunting techniques to the kind of individual stalking and selective control which rifle hunting allows. Traditional pre-firearm Inuvialuit caribou hunting, like that of other Inuit, was based on drives and ambushes (MacFarlane 1905; Stefansson 1914; Pullen 1979: 101). Modified catastrophic mortality profiles from Rita-Claire and Bison Skull are in keeping with these kinds of hunting strategies, which offer little selective control on the part of the hunter.

Sex

Like most mammals, caribou exhibit some sexual dimorphism. Most general measurements of size and weight (Banfield 1961, 1974: 385; Miller 1974; see also Speiss 1979) suggest about a one-standard-deviation difference between male and female modes, so that frequency distributions generally present a single bell curve, with males occupying the larger end of the graph and females the smaller, with some degree of overlap. Several sets of osteometric data have been proposed for distinguishing sex in archaeological samples. One is based on mandibular measurements (Morrison and Whitridge 1997), and another on the dimensions of the epiphyseal ends of metapodials (Gronnow et al. 1983; Stenton 1989, 1991). Both present similar problems.

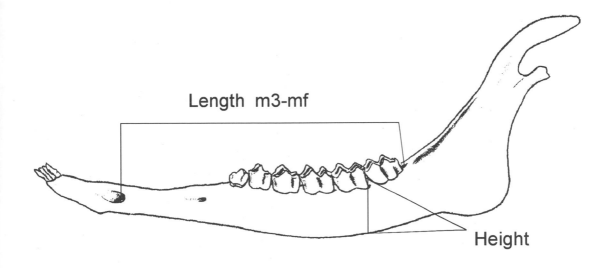

Figure 5.6. Mandibular measurements used for inferring sex.

Mandibular Measurements

In his 1974 study of the Kaminuriak herd, Miller found that sex could be accurately inferred from overall mandibular length, particularly for animals five years of age and older (Miller 1974: Fig. 20). Unfortunately, complete caribou mandibles are exceedingly rare in archaeological assemblages, and some smaller measurement is clearly required for archaeological purposes. Morrison and Whitridge (1997) experimented with several using their Kaminuriak control sample, including diastema and tooth-row lengths. Meaningful results, however, were obtained for only two; *length,* measured from the rear of the third molar alveolus to the mental foramen (m3-mf), and the maximum *height* of the corpus, measured between m2 and m3 (Fig. 5.6). Together they achieved acceptable results, yielding the following linear discriminant function

discriminant score = 0.319 * height (in mm.) + 0.169 * length (in mm) - 35.647

Any case with a discriminant score greater than or equal to zero is classified as male, and cases with a score less than zero as female, with an apparent error rate of 23% due to overlap. The closer to zero a particular discriminant score is, the less certain its sexual identification.

Only two independent mandibles in each of the three Rita-Claire and Bison Skull assemblages was complete enough to produce results using this formula. Results are presented in Table 5.2. In each case, one mandible produced a discriminant score greater than 0, suggesting - all other things being equal - a male, while the other produced a score of less than 0, suggesting a female. However, all but two specimens produced discriminant scores within 0.6 of the 0 line, and their identification is far from certain.

It seems clear that over and above any inherent methodological problems, this technique of sexing suffers from a serious practical consideration, due to the rarity of even partially intact mandibles in many archaeological components. A more general criticism is considered later in this discussion.

Metapodial Measurements

Gronnow et al. (1983) and Stenton (1991) have both published control-sample data on metapodial measurements which they have used to infer the sexual structure of archaeological caribou assemblages in the Eastern Arctic. Each presents scatterplots graphing distal condylar height against breadth — Gronnow et al. for metatarsals and Stenton for both metacarpals and metatarsals — without presenting the actual measurements themselves, nor any statistical analysis of the results. No discriminant line is defined and the degree of overlap is not specified mathematically. Archaeological results are merely sorted by placing them on the same grid as the control sample, and visually assessing where they fall. This procedure is less unsatisfactory than it might seem, however, since the degree of overlap between males and females in the control samples is very slight, less than was the case with mandibles (Gronnow et al. 1983: Fig. 79; Stenton 1991: Fig. 9 and 10). Moreover, distal metapodials are generally far better represented in archaeological contexts than are relatively complete mandibles, so sample size tends to be large and, presumably, relatively representative.

Distal metapodials from the Rita-Claire and Bison Skull sites were measured for comparative purposes. Following Stenton (1989: 279), the precise measurements employed are those codified as numbers 121 and 123 by Speiss (1979: Fig. 3-5): i.e. condylar breadth across the distal end of the epiphysis, and maximum anterior-posterior height, again measured across the condyles (Fig. 5.7).

Speiss (1979: 86-88) has suggested that for measurements such as these it is acceptable to include unfused epiphyses from all but the very youngest individuals, since epiphyseal dimensions aside from total length are not affected by growth and fusion. Stenton (1989: 279) has accepted this suggestion, while Gronnow et al. (1983) are silent on the subject. However, as it is based on only very

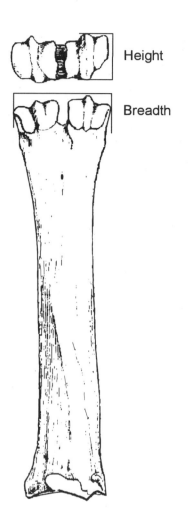

Height

Breadth

Figure 5.7. Distal metapodial measurements used for inferring sex.

Table 5.2. Discriminant scores.

Site	"Male"	"Female"
Rita-Claire	4.56	-0.55
Bison Skull West	0.21	-1.26
Bison Skull East	0.05	-0.29

Table 5.3: Fused vs. Unfused Distal Metapodial Measurements

Variable	Unfused Metacarpal	Fused Metacarpal	Unfused Metatarsal	Fused Metatarsal
Number of specimens	11	24	15	16
Mean height (mm)	22.3	23.0	23.3	24.0
Mean breadth (mm)	42.0	43.6	41.5	42.5

general information, it needs to be considered more fully before both fused and unfused epiphyses are included in the study sample.

Table 5.3 presents the means for height and breadth measurements for fused and unfused distal metapodial epiphyses, based on the total Rita-Claire and Bison Skull sample of 25 metacarpals and 31 metatarsals (these figures ignore specimens too eroded or damaged to be measured). As can be seen, in the case of both metacarpals and metatarsals, unfused epiphyses are smaller than fused epiphyses in both dimensions by 2%-3%. Independent t-tests indicate that this difference hovers on or just over the edge of statistical significance. For metacarpals, the probability that fused and unfused distal epiphyses are identical for height is 0.035, while for breadth it is 0.050. For metatarsals, the probabilities for height and breadth are 0.092 and 0.057. Considering how slight sexual variation is in caribou, it would probably be prudent to exclude measurements based on unfused epiphyses.

Figures 5.8 and 5.9 graph height and breadth dimensions for fused distal metapodials from the Rita-Claire and Bison Skull sites against Stenton's (1991: Fig. 9 and 10) control data. This control as chosen over that of Gronnow et al. (1983) because it is based on a larger sample (46 vs 23 individuals), comes from a less distant geographic area (Baffin Island vs west Greenland) and includes both metatarsals and metacarpals. A visual assessment of the metatarsal distribution presented by Gronnow et al. (1983: Fig. 79), however, suggests no significant dimensional difference compared with that of Stenton.

Results from the two elements are not consistent. Taking the Rita-Claire and Bison Skull sample as a whole, or focussing exclusively on Rita-Claire (the Bison Skull sample is too small to be considered independently), it seems that just over half of the metatarsals are female (9 of 16 of the pooled sample), while most metacarpals are male (18 of 24). Part of the discrepency may be due to the fact that discriminant lines are visual fits only and many specimens fall within a potential area of overlap. Moreover, neither the metacarpals nor the metatarsals represent independent samples. Distal metapodials cannot usually be accurately sided (it depends on how much shaft is attached), and so each specimen may not exclusively represent an individual animal. An examination of the metatarsal scattergram (Fig. 5.9), however, suggests a third and probably more generally important variable, one that pertains to both metapodial and mandibular measurements.

The Problem of Geographic Variation

Judging by present population distributions, the Rita-Claire and Bison Skull caribou are conspecific with animals in the Kaminuriak herd, and also with the animals from which Stenton (1991) and Gronnow et al. (1983) derived their control samples. All are members of the subspecies *Rangifer tarandus groenlandicus*, the barrenground caribou (Banfield 1961; Kelsall 1968). Unfortunately for present purposes, this subspecies is a very widespread one, encompassing a considerable range in morphological variation. Variation in size has a mosaic-like distribution in space (Banfield 1961: 54), and probably in time as well, an observation which should cast a considerable pall over attempts to infer sex on the basis of

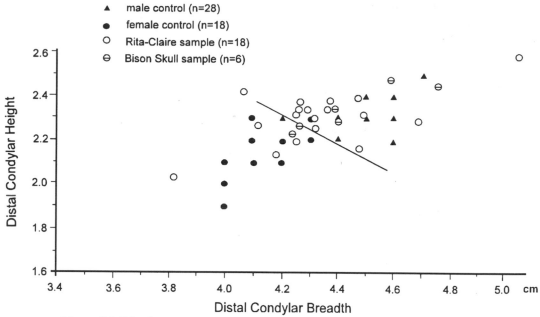

Figure 5.8. Distal metacarpal measurements (controls after Stenton 1991: Fig. 10).

minor differences in mandibular or metapodial dimensions.

That this is so seems likely even when comparing the archaeological and control data. Mandibular size was first used in an attempt to infer sex at two archaeological sites close to and roughly contemporaneous with Rita-Claire and Bison Skull (Morrison and Whitridge 1997). Independent t-test indicated that the archaeological specimens were significantly larger than the Kaminuriak control specimens. Conversely, an examination of Stenton's (1991: Tables 9 and 10) scattergrams strongly suggest that his archaeological specimens are significantly *smaller* than the control specimens. It may of course be that the archaeological specimens were selected - by ancient hunters - for their size, so that most of Stenton's specimens are, as he suggests, female. But it seems at least as likely than the population they were derived from was itself morphologically smaller than his modern control sample.

A similar situation may be suspected with the Rita-Claire and Bison Skull metatarsal measurements (Fig. 5.9). The archaeological specimens overlap well with Stenton's control sample with regard to breadth, but fairly consistently present a greater condylar height. It would seem unwarranted to apply a discriminant line based on one sample to infer sex in another when they are of dissimilar morphological size.

What then of situations where the control sample and the archaeological sample are not obviously dissimilar? Several examples can be cited, including Gronnow's metatarsal comparison from west Greenland (Gronnow et al. 1983: Fig. 79), and the metacarpal comparison presented in this study (Fig. 5.8). Can they be accepted as valid inferences of sex? Not necessarily.

We know the frequency of males and females in the control sample. We do not know how the archaeological sample was selected; indeed this is very thing we are trying to find out. It may be, for instance, that ancient hunters were selecting males almost

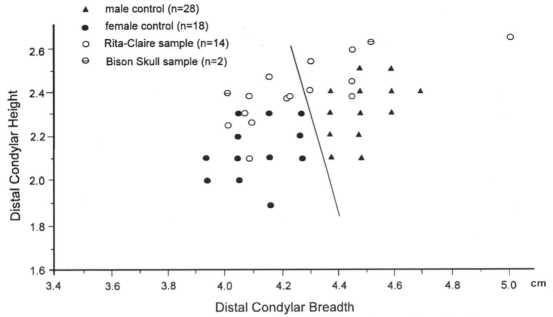

Figure 5.9. Distal metatarsal measurements (controls after Stenton 1991: Fig. 9).

exclusively, but that the population from which they were selecting them was morphologically smaller than the control sample. This could result in an archaeological sample which was similar in morphological size and even range to a more sexually-balanced control sample. Clearly the size distinction between males and females in the control sample could have no relevance to the archaeological sample, where we can never investigate morphological size independently from selection.

In short, caribou are not sexually dimorphic enough, considering the range of geographic and perhaps temporal variation they encompass, for the sexes to be validly distinguished by size in an archaeological context.

Chapter 6 —————————————————————————

Conclusions

"One thing that Binford proved with Nunamiut Ethnoarchaeology *is that the past would be much easier to figure out if we had only been there to watch it."* (Roscoe Wilmeth)

In many areas of Arctic North America, most unsolved culture-historical problems are of apparently minor significance or depend for their solving on particular and unusual kinds of discoveries. Many archaeological sites yield familiar tool kits with familiar cultural associations, and present few if any surprises in their artifact inventories. In such situations the analysis of one more artifact collection has (or at least seems to have) little potential for advancing our knowledge of the past. It is within this kind of context that the enormous growth and elaboration of zooarchaeology has occurred within the past two decades, as archaeologists begin looking intensively at their other major data source. The past few chapters give some indication of just how great and elaborate this growth has been.

The present study was undertaken with two major goals in mind. One was to provide comparative data and explore the usefulness of various analytical tests concerned with the interpretation of caribou faunas in general, the other to explore caribou use at two particular archaeological sites on the Cape Bathurst Peninsula. To what extent have these goals been realized? Zooarchaeological analysis is a highly labour-intensive activity. Does analysis beyond the level of mere identification really tell us much that was not already apparent (or assumed) about the economic patterns and practises of ancient hunters?

General Considerations

At a general level, some progress in the study of caribou archaeofaunas can be claimed. Attempts at establishing the age and season of death of animals based on tooth eruption and wear have been largely successful, although some interpretative difficulties remain. The analysis of bone fragmentation and breakage patterns has proved informative of past economic practises, especially (in the present context) those relating to marrow cracking and possibly butchering. Some insights into general economic situation have been advanced based on the intensiveness of marrow cracking and of juvenile caribou use, and attempts have been made to model anatomical-part frequency signatures in relation to site use. Having sites or site components which represent a range of uses has assisted in a comparative approach, with some of the more specific results described below.

Continuing problems and difficulties, however, abound. It is probably fair to say that the factors conditioning the makeup of most faunal assemblages have proved (and not only in this study) far more numerous and complex than may have been hoped. The utility index approach pioneered by Binford (1978), for instance, has been seriously compromised by the discovery that the original "transported" composition of an assemblage can be (and usually is) obscured by subsequent taphonomic processes (Lyman 1994a), of which carnivore gnawing seems perhaps the most ubiquitous. Many attempts to sort out these processes, especially those which are density mediated, have also proved inadequate, focussing on a few not necessarily representative skeletal elements, or employing graphic tests which assume what they are attempting to demonstrate. Attempts to infer sex and hence sexual selection on the part of ancient hunters are also thwarted, in the case of caribou, by a relatively low degree of sexual dimorphism and a relatively high degree of geographic variation.

Aside from taphonomy, an important problem to be stressed with regard to utility indices is their static and quite possibly mis-leading nature. The relative nutritional value of different anatomical parts varies with nutritional state, and hence to some extent seasonally. This variability cannot be captured in a static utility index. Moreover, the basic utility index, the MGUI, is based overwhelmingly on meat weight, where ethnographic evidence indicates that traditional hunters were themselves concerned almost exclusively with fat. There are fat utility indices — specifically for bone grease and marrow — but the whole issue clearly needs to be re-thought.

Several other often poorly recognized factors can also obscure the quality of information which faunal material can convey. One of these is the palimpsest effect, whereby material from different occupational episodes is lumped together in a single analytical unit in even the most carefully excavated site (Grayson 1984). Recent calls to consider as distinct aggregation units the different architectural portions of a Neoeskimo house (Stenton and Park 1994) are a useful attempt

to control this situation, at least with regard to Neoeskimo houses. However, some degree of lumping is still inevitable in almost any site which has been occupied more than once, as most Inuit sites over the past thousand years seem to have been (see Park 1997).

What has been referred to as "over-writing" is another and equally difficult problem. Bones are not simply brought into an archaeological site for some "utilitarian" purpose and then abandoned to taphonomic destruction. Instead, they are often used and re-used, processed and re-processed in a number of different ways. In so doing, one processing activity may obscure another; tool manufacture may obscure evidence of marrow cracking (both may focus on metapodials), and bones brought into a site primarily for their attached meat may then be processed for their bone grease. Some uses can be entirely destructive, depending in part upon the identification skills of the analyst, while others are not. What are we to make of bone grease utility, for instance, which can be a positive factor in conditioning which elements are brought into a site, but then a negative one in conditioning what survives in recognizable form? The fact that several utility indices are statistically related to each other can be a further source of confusion.

In the end, many of the complexities of faunal use and preservation at sites like Rita-Claire and Bison Skull seem beyond unravelling, at least with present analytical methods. Whether the attempt is worth the labour is a matter for individual judgement, but without such attempts the kinds of problems we have examined will remain unresolved. Faunal remains are the most abundant class of items in many archaeological sites, and faunal analysis still offers enormous potential for understanding the past.

Inuvialuit Caribou Hunting
on Cape Bathurst

Turning from the general to the particular, faunal analysis suggests a number of conclusions and tentative generalizations concerning the economic activities undertaken at Rita-Claire and Bison Skull, and the place these sites occupied within the local subsistence economy. We can examine these conclusions one by one.

1. Both sites and all three components were occupied or utilized in conjunction with the autumn caribou hunt. Evidently many precontact Inuvialuit depended heavily on caribou for at least part of their annual cycle, as one would expect from later historic accounts. Caribou hunters lived in temporary, open-air camps located inland from, but probably tethered to, coastal winter villages.

2. Hunting focussed on cooperative, communal techniques which allowed relatively little selective control over the age (and presumably the sex) of animals being killed. Drives like those described historically were probably operated in conjunction with various ambush strategies, such as the shooting blinds at Bison Skull East.

3. Under mass-kill conditions, as represented by Bison Skull West, initial butchering and processing seems to have been strongly structured spatially, in a manner similar to that recorded from bison kill sites on the Great Plains (e.g. Wheat 1972; Frison and Todd 1987). Bone beds of the size of Bison Skull West, however, are not typical of any area of the Arctic. Most traditional caribou kills are much smaller, and have a very low archaeological visibility; for instance, no primary butchering area was found associated with the shooting blinds at Bison Skull East.

4. There is no evidence of bone-grease manufacture at any of the components, and as a practise it seems to be generally rare in Inuit culture. There may have been technological constraints, including the absence of stone boiling, the small size of traditional vessels, and problems with access to fuel. It is likely, too, that most Inuit had sufficient access to sea mammal fat to make the laborious rendering of bone grease unnecessary under normal conditions (except perhaps as a high status "treat" food).

5. Habitation sites associated with caribou hunting exhibit highly fragmented bone assemblages, although not as highly fragmented as some Great Plains bison bone assemblages where bone grease manufacture was practised. Look-out/kill and especially mass-kill butchering sites exhibit lower degrees of fragmentation, in keeping with simpler use patterns.

6. Density-mediated factors, particularly carnivore gnawing, are probably the most important factors conditioning the composition of most Arctic faunal assemblages, including Rita-Claire and Bison Skull East. These factors may be most operative at habitation sites.

7. The Inuvialuit kept dogs at autumn habitation sites like Rita-Claire, where they were fed caribou scraps and probably closely tied. As much as possible dogs were not allowed on look-out/kill locations.

8. Marrow cracking was an important activity at habitation sites like Rita-Claire, and may be a particular signature of look-out/kill sites like Bison Skull East. Anatomical part frequencies are not necessarily the best guide to this, first because there is a highly significant correlation between marrow utility and volume density, and second because the

relationship between transportation and cracking can be a very complicated one. The frequency of marrow bones brought into a look-out/kill site for "snacking" purposes, for instance, is heavily conditioned by their availability in the habitation site from which the look-out/kill was operated.

9. The degree of marrow cracking practised by the inhabitants of a site like Rita-Claire is great enough to suggest some degree of food stress, at least measured by modern standards. Pre-gun, pre-fur trade Inuit were probably more generally frugal than their more recent descendants.

10. As among more recent Inuit, the inhabitants of the Rita-Claire site preferred to eat the heads of younger and/or female caribou rather than those of adult males. The taste for calves, however, did not extend to bone marrow; despite the extensive cracking of adult marrow bones, few immature bones were cracked. This observation may suggest that traditional Inuit frugality had its limits, at least in situations of temporary plenty.

This study has examined the Rita-Claire and Bison Skull sites mainly in terms of the autumn season during which they were occupied. But autumn caribou-hunting sites were also part of a larger seasonal round, and a larger social world, observations which must have implications when considering faunal inventories. In ethnographically described Inuit economies generally, the autumn caribou hunt was a crucial provisioning time, when surplus meat and hides were "banked" for winter (Burch 1972) or even spring (MacFarlane 1905: 681) consumption. In an incipiently ranked society like the Inuvialuit, we can also suspect that social roles, wealth, and status may have differed for groups which spent the autumn in the intensive hunting of caribou, while others concentrated instead on

whale hunting from coastal villages (see Morrison 1988). A question for further research, and further consideration, is how do we investigate this relationship between interior provisioning sites like Rita-Claire and Bison Skull, and the permanent coastal villages with which they were associated?

Two inter-related issues are food storage, and the transportation of stored food (or food to be stored) away from provisioning sites. Transportation either by umiak (in summer) or dog sled (in winter) is a simple matter, and may have required little processing to reduce weight or bulk. Food storage techniques, too, need not have been elaborate. Autumn weather is chilly if not yet actually cold, and hard frosts increasingly frequent. It would probably not be necessary smoke meat, a still common summer-time practise in the Inuvialuit area, and one leaving clear archaeological traces as well (see Morrison 1994). Instead, drying and simple cold storage would probably suffice, either in caches or on meat platforms, both of which have been found archaeologically in association with late autumn and winter houses (e.g. Morrison 1988). Thus far, the contents of only a single Inuvialuit cache have been described in print (Morrison 1988: 27), and it was a small "convenience" cache quite distinct from the much larger, log-lined cache pits described historically (Miertsching 1967: 55; Nagy 1994: 97). Disappointingly, its contents appear to have consisted of garbage rather than primary stored food. The analysis of further cache contents — if and when an intact cache is identified and excavated — and caribou remains from exclusively winter sites would go a long way toward helping to model selection for dried or frozen storage. A careful consideration of Binford's (1978) discussion of Nunamiut dried and frozen storage might also be fruitful.

An investigation of the relationship between provisioning and main village sites must of course consider both halves of the relationship. The excavation and analysis of large coastal villages should proceed with this goal, doubtless one of many. Are faunal assemblages relatively uniform, or do different houses or house clusters within a site contain significantly different proportions of terrestrial and sea mammal bone? If status differentiation is apparent, how does this relate to terrestrial and maritime faunal representation? Can it be determined whether terrestrial resources were obtained locally, or from distant provisioning sites?

Unfortunately, in the Cape Bathurst area permanent coastal villages have been all but destroyed by coastal subsidence. Other large Inuvialuit villages remain, particularly in the Mackenzie Delta area (Arnold 1994), so these questions are not at least generally unsolvable. However it may be, it seems very likely that an additional reason why the Rita-Claire caribou fauna makes so little sense in terms of utility is that a good portion of it is missing, hauled off to now-vanished coastal villages for winter consumption.

References Cited

Andrews, Peter. 1990. *Owls, Caves and Fossils*. Chicago: University of Chicago Press.

Arnold, Charles. 1994. Archaeological investigations on Richards Island. In, *Bridges Across Time: The NOGAP Archaeology Project*, J.L. Pilon, ed., pp. 85-94. Canadian Archaeological Assocation, Occasional Paper No. 2.

Balkwill, Darlene. 1987. An Arctic cornucopia: faunal diversity at the Saunaktuk site, NWT. Paper presented at the 20th annual meetings of the Canadian Archaeological Association, Calgary.

Balkwill, Darlene and Anne Rick. 1994. Siglit Subsistence: preliminary report on faunal remains from a large midden at the Gupuk site (NiTs-1), Mackenzie Delta, NWT. In, *Bridges Across Time: The NOGAP Archaeology Project*, J.-L. Pilon, ed., pp. 95-116. Canadian Archaeological Association, Occasional Paper 2.

Banfield, A.W.F. 1961. A Revision of the Reindeer and Caribou, Genus *Rangifer*. *National Museum of Canada Bulletin*, 177.

Banfield, A.W.F. 1974. *The Mammals of Canada*. Toronto: University of Toronto Press.

Barnes, Frank. 1980. *Cartridges of the World*, 4th edition. Northfield, IL.: DBI Books.

Behrensmeyer, Anna K. 1978. Taphonomic and ecologic information from bone weathering. *Paloeobiology*, 4(2): 150-162.

Binford, Lewis. 1978. *Nunamiut Ethnoarchaeology*. New York: Academic Press.

Binford, Lewis. 1979. Organization and formation processes: looking at curated technologies. *Journal of Anthropological Research*, 35: 255-273.

Binford, Lewis. 1981. *Bones: Ancient Men and Modern Myths*. New York: Academic Press.

Binford, Lewis. 1984. *Faunal Remains from Klaises River Mouth*. New York: Academic Press.

Binford, Lewis and Jack Bertram. 1977. Bone frequencies and attritional processes. In, *For Theory Building in Archaeology*, L. Binford, ed., pp. 77-153. New York: Academic Press.

Birket-Smith, Kaj. 1929. *The Caribou Eskimos*. Report of the Fifth Thule Expedition, 1921-24, 5(1).

Bockstoce, John. 1986. *Whales, Ice, and Men: The history of whaling in the western Arctic*. Seattle: University of Washington Press.

Brink, Jack and Bob Dawe. 1989. *Final Report of the 1985 and 1986 Field Season at Head-Smashed-In Buffalo Jump, Alberta*. Edmonton: Archaeo-logical Survey of Alberta Manuscript Series, 16.

Burch, Ernest S. 1972. The Caribou/Wild Reindeer as Human Resource. *American Antiquity*, 37(3): 339-368.

Burch, Ernest S. 1991. Review of "The Kugaluk Site and the Nuvorugmiut," by D. Morrison. *Canadian Journal of Archaeology*, 15: 266-270.

Davis, James, Patrick Valkenburg and Daniel Reed. 1987. Correlations and depletion patterns of marrow fat in caribou bones.

Journal of Wildlife Management, 51(2): 365-371.

Driver, Jonathan C. 1992. Identification, classification, and zooarchaeology. *Circaea*, 9(1): 35-47.

Dyck, Ian and Richard Morlan. 1995. *The Sjovold Site: A river crossing campsite in the northern Plains*. Canadian Museum of Civilization, Mercury Series, Archaeological Survey of Canada Paper 151.

Fraker, Mark and John Bockstoce. 1980. Summer distribution of bowhead whales in the eastern Beaufort Sea. *Marine Fisheries Review*, 42(9-10): 57-64.

Freeman, Milton M. 1976. *Inuit Land Use and Occupancy Project, Volume 3: Land Use Atlas*. Ottawa: Department of Indian and Northern Affairs.

Frison, George C. and L.C.Todd (eds.). 1987. *The Horner Site: The type site of the Cody cultural complex*. Orlando, Fla.: Academic Press.

Godfrey, Earl. 1986. *The Birds of Canada*. Ottawa: National Museum of Natural Sciences.

Gronnow, Bjarne, Morten Meldgaard and Jorn Nielsen. 1983. *Aasivissuit - The Great Summer Camp: Archaeological, ethnographical and zoo-archaeological studies of a caribou-hunting site in West Greenland*. Meddelelser om Gronland, Man and Society, 5.

Grayson, Donald. 1984. *Quantative Zoo-archaeology: Topics in the analysis of archaeological faunas*. Orlando, Fla.: Academic Press,

Grayson, Donald. 1989. Bone Transport, Bone Destruction, and Reverse Utility Curves. *Journal of Archaeological Science*, 16: 643-652.

Hall, Judy, Jill Oakes and Sally Qimmiu'naaq

Webster. 1994. *Sanatujut: Pride in Women's Work*. Hull, P.Q.: Canadian Museum of Civilization.

Harington, C.R. 1980. Radiocarbon dates on some Quaternary mammals and artifacts from northern North America. *Arctic*, 33(4): 815-832.

Harington, C.R. 1990. Arctic Bison. *Biome*, 10(2): 4.

Jenness, Diamond. 1922. *The Life of the Copper Eskimos*. Report of the Canadian Arctic Expedition, 1913-18, vol. 12a.

Jenness, Diamond. 1946. *Material Culture of the Copper Eskimo*. Report of the Canadian Arctic Expedition, 1913-18, vol. 16.

Jones, K.T. and D. Metcalfe. 1988. Bare Bones Archaeology: Bone Marrow Indices and Efficiency. *Journal of Archaeological Science*, 15: 415-423.

Kelsall, J. 1968. The Migratory Barren-Ground Caribou of Canada. *Canadian Wildlife Service, Monograph*, 3.

Klein, Richard and K. Cruz-Uribe. 1984. *The Analysis of Animal Bones from Archaeological Sites*. Chicago: University of Chicago Press.

Klein, Richard, C. Wolf, L. G. Freeman and K. Allwarden. 1981. The use of dental crown heights for constructing age profiles of red deer and similar species in archaeological samples. *Journal of Archaeological Science*, 8: 1-31.

Klein, Richard, K. Allwarden, and C. Wolf. 1983. The calculation and interpretation of ungulate age profiles from dental crown heights. In, *Hunter-Gatherer Economy in Prehistory: A European Perspective*, G. Bailey, ed., pp. 47-57. Cambridge: Cambridge University Press.

Le Blanc, Raymond. n.d. Archaeological research in the Mackenzie Delta region. Ms 3059, on file with the Canadian Museum of

Civilization, Hull, P.Q.

Le Blanc, Raymond. 1994. *The Crane Site and the Palaeoeskimo. Period in the Western Canadian Arctic*. Canadian Museum of Civilization, Archaeological Survey of Canada, Mercury Series Paper 148.

Lyman, R. Lee. 1984. Bone density and differential survivorship of fossil classes. *Journal of Anthropological Archaeology*, 3: 259-299.

Lyman, R. Lee. 1985. Bone frequencies: differential survivorship of fossil classes. *Journal of Archaeological Science*, 12: 221-236.

Lyman, R. Lee. 1991. Taphonomic Problems with Archaeological Analyses of Animal Carcass Utilization and Transport. In, *Beamers, Bobwhites, and Blue-Points: Tributes to the Career of Paul W. Parmalee*, J. Purdue, W. Klippel, and B. Styles, Eds. Illinois State Museum Scientific Papers, 23, and the University of Tennessee, Department of Anthropology Report of Investigations, 52, pp. 125-138.

Lyman, R. Lee. 1994a. *Vertebrate Taphonomy*. Cambridge: Cambridge University Press.

Lyman, R. Lee. 1994b. Quantitative units and terminology in zooarchaeology. *American Antiquity* 59(1): 36-71.

MacFarlane, Roderick. 1905. Notes on mammals collected and observed in the northern Mackenzie River District, Northwest Territories of Canada. *Proceedings of the U.S. National Museum*, 28: 673-764.

Mackay, J. Ross. 1958. *The Anderson River Map Area, N.W.T.* Department of Mines and Technical Surveys, Geographical Branch, Memoir 5.

Mackay, J. Ross. 1981. Dating the Horton River breakthrough, District of Mackenzie. Current Research Part 8, pp. 129-132, *Geological Survey of Canada Paper*, 81-1b.

Marean, Curtis and Lillian Spencer. 1991. Impact of carnivore ravaging on zooarchaeological measures of element abundance. *American Antiquity*, 56(4):645-658.

Martell, A., D. Dickinson and L. Casselman. 1984. *Wildlife of the Mackenzie Delta Region*. Boreal Institute for Northern Studies, Occasional Publication 15.

M'Clure, Robert. 1969. *The Discovery of the North-West Passage*, S. Osborn, ed. Edmonton: Hurtig.

McGhee, Robert. 1974. *Beluga Hunters: An Archaeological Reconstruction of the History and Culture of the Mackenzie Delta Kittegaryumiut*. Memorial University of Newfoundland, Newfoundland Social and Economic Studies, 13.

Metcalfe, D. and K.T. Jones. 1988. A reconsideration of animal body-part utility indices. *American Antiquity*, 53: 486-504.

Miertsching, Johann. 1967. *Frozen Ships: The arctic diary of Johann Miertsching*, L. Neatby, translator. TorontoL Macmillan.

Miller, Frank. 1974. Biology of the Kaminuriak Population of Barren-Ground Caribou, Part 2. *Canadian Wildlife Service, Report Series*, 31.

Morlan, Richard E. 1994. Bison bone fragmentation and survivorship: a comparative method. *Journal of Archaeological Science*, 21, pp. 797-807.

Morrison, David. 1983. *Thule Culture in Western Coronation Gulf, N.W.T.* National Museum of Man, Mercury Series, Archaeological Survey of Canada Paper 116.

Morrison, David. 1986. Inuit and Kutchin bone and antler industries in northwestern Canada. *Canadian Journal of Archaeology*, 10: 107-123.

Morrison, David. 1988. *The Kugaluk Site and the Nuvorugmiut*. Canadian Museum of Civilization, Mercury Series, Archaeological

Survey of Canada Paper 137.

Morrison, David. 1990. *Iglulualumiut Prehistory: The lost Inuit of Franklin Bay.* Canadian Museum of Civilization, Mercury Series, Archaeological Survey of Canada Paper 142.

Morrison, David. 1991. The Copper Inuit soapstone trade. *Arctic,* vol. 44: 239-246.

Morrison, David. 1994. An archaeological perspective on Neoeskimo economies. In, *Threads of Arctic Prehistory: Papers in Honour of William E. Taylor, Jr.,* D. Morrison and J.L. Pilon, eds., pp. 311-324. Canadian Museum of Civilization, Mercury Series, Archaeological Survey of Canada Paper. No. 149.

Morrison, David. in press. An ethnohistory of the Inuvialuit from earliest times to 1902. *Revista de Arqueologia Americana.*

Morrison, David and Charles Arnold. 1994. The Inuktuiut of the Eskimo Lakes. In, *Bridges Across Time: The NOGAP Archaeology Project,* J.L. Pilon, ed., pp. 117-126. Canadian Archaeological Assocation, Occasional Paper No. 2.

Morrison, David and Peter Whitridge. 1997. Estimating the age and sex of caribou from mandibular measurements. *Journal of Archaeological Science,* 24:

Munson, P. 1991. Mortality profiles of white-tailed deer from archaeological sites in eastern North America: selective hunting or taphonomy? In, *Beamers, Bobwhites, and Blue-Points: Tributes to the Career of Paul W. Parmalee,* J. Purdue, W. Klippel, and B. Styles, eds. Illinois State Museum Scientific Papers, 23, and the University of Tennessee, Department of Anthropology Report of Investigations, 52, pp. 139-152.

Murdoch, John. 1988 (orig. 1892*). Ethnological Results of the Point Barrow Expedition.* Washington: Smithsonian Institution Press.

Nagy, Murielle. 1990. *Caribou Exploitation at the Trail River Site.* Heritage Branch, Government of the Yukon, Occasional Papers in Archaeology, 2.

Nagy, Murielle. 1994. *Yukon North Slope Inuvialuit Oral History.* Heritage Branch, Government of the Yukon, Occasional Papers in Yukon History, No. 1.

Park, Robert. 1997. Thule winter site demography in the High Arctic. *American Antiquity* 62(2): 273-284.

Pilon, Jean-Luc. 1990. Vihtr'iitshik: A stone quarry reported by Alexander Mackenzie on the lower Mackenzie River in 1789. *Arctic,* 43(3): 251-261.

Pullen, H.F. 1979. *The Pullen Expedition.* Toronto: Arctic History Press.

Rainey, Froelich. 1947. *The Whale Hunters of Tigara.* Anthropological Papers of the American Museum of Natural History, 41(2).

Rampton, Vern N. 1988. *Quaternary Geology of the Tuktoyaktuk Coastlands, Northwest Territories.* Geological Survey of Canada, Memoir 423.

Reeves, B.O.K. 1990. Communal bison hunters of the Northern Plains. In, *Hunters of the Recent Past,* L.B. Davis and B. Reeves, eds., pp. 168-194. London: Unwin Hyman.

Reher, Charles. 1974. Population study of the Casper site bison. In, *The Casper Site,* G. Frison, ed., pp. 113-124. New York: Academic Press.

Reher, Charles and George Frison. 1980. The Vore Site, 48CK302, a Stratified Buffalo Jump in the Wyoming Black Hills. *Plains Anthropologist, Memoir,* 16.

Richardson, John. 1851. *Arctic Searching Expedition,* Vol. 1. London: Longmans, Brown, Green, and Longmans.

Richardson, P.R.K. 1980. Carnivore damage on antelope bones and its archaeological implications. *Paleontologia Africana*, 23: 109-125.

Rick, Anne. 1975. Bird medullary bone: a seasonal dating technique for faunal analysis. *Canadian Archaeological Association, Bulletin*, 7: 183-190.

Ringrose, T.J. 1993. Bone counts and statistics: a critique. *Journal of Archaeological Science*, 20: 121-157.

Savoie, Donat. 1970. *The Amerindians of the Canadian Northwest in the 19th Century, as Seen by Emile Petitot, Vol. 1: The Tchiglit Eskimos*. Mackenzie Delta Research Project 9.

Schledermann, Peter. 1990. *Crossroads to Greenland: 3000 Years of Prehistory in the Eastern High Arctic*. The Arctic Institute of North America of the University of Calgary, Komatik Series, 2.

Schwarz, Herbert. 1970. *Elik, and other stories of the Mackenzie Eskimos*. Toronto: McClelland and Stewart.

Scott, William B. and E.J. Crossman. 1973. *Freshwater fishes of Canada*. Ottawa: Fisheries Research Board of Canada.

Siegel, Sidney. 1956. *Nonparametric Statistics for the Behavioural Sciences*. New York: McGraw Hill.

Speiss, Arthur. 1979. *Reindeer and Caribou Hunters: an archaeological study*. New York: Academic Press.

Spencer, Robert. 1959. *The North Alaskan Eskimo: A Study in Ecology and Society*. Bureau of American Ethnology Bulletin, 171.

Speth, J. 1983. *Bison Kills and Bone Counts: Decision Making by Ancient Hunters*. Chicago: University of Chicago Press.

Speth, J. 1991. Taphonomy and Early Hominid Behaviour: problems in distinguishing cultural and non-cultural agents. In, *Human Predators and Prey Mortality*, M. Stiner, ed., pp. 31-40. Boulder, Colorado: Westview Press.

Stefansson, Vilhjalmur. 1914. *The Stefansson-Anderson Arctic Expedition: Preliminary Ethnographic Results*. Anthropological Papers of the American Museum of Natural History, 14(1).

Stefansson, Vilhjalmur. 1946. *Not By Bread Alone*. New York: Macmillan.

Stefansson, Vilhjalmur. 1962 (orig. 1913). *My Life with the Eskimo*. New York: Collier.

Stenton, Douglas. 1989. Terrestrial Adaptations of Neo-Eskimo Coastal-Marine Hunters on Southern Baffin Island, NWT. Unpublished PhD dissertation, University of Alberta, Edmonton.

Stenton, Douglas. 1991. Caribou population dynamics and Thule culture adaptations on southern Baffin Island, NWT. *Arctic Anthropology*, 28(2): 15-43.

Stenton, Douglas and Robert Park. 1994. Formation processes and Thule archaeo-faunas. In, *Threads of Arctic Prehistory: Papers in Honour of William E. Taylor, Jr.*, D. Morrison and J.L. Pilon, eds., pp. 409-422. Canadian Museum of Civilization, Mercury Series, Archaeological Survey of Canada Paper. No. 149.

Still, Leslie. 1996a. Avian fauna from the Rita-Claire site OaRw-3. Ms on file with the Canadian Museum of Civilization, Hull, P.Q.

Still, Leslie. 1996b. Bony fish remains from the Rita-Claire site (OaRw-3). Ms on file with the Canadian Museum of Civilizaiton, Hull, P.Q.

Still, Leslie. 1996c. Bird and bony fish remains from OaRw-2, Bison Skull I and II. Ms on file with the Canadian Museum of Civilization, Hull. P.Q.

Stiner, Mary (ed.). 1991. *Human Predators and Prey Mortality*. Boulder, Colorado: Westview Press.

Stone, A.J. 1900. Some results of a natural history journey to northern British Columbia, Alaska, and the Northwest Territory. *American Museum of Natural History, Bulletin* XIII, pp. 31-62.

Swayze, Ken. 1994. The Tuktoyaktuk Peninsula interior: pre-contact Inuvialuit landuse. In, *Bridges Across Time: The NOGAP Archaeology Project*, J.L. Pilon, ed., pp. 127-150. Canadian Archaeological Assocation, Occasional Paper 2.

Thomas, David H. 1969. Great Basin hunting patterns: a quantitative method for treating faunal remains. *American Antiquity*, 34(4): 392-401.

Thomas, David H. and D. Mayer. 1983. Behavioral Faunal Analysis of Selected Horizons. In *The Archaeology of Monitor Valley 2, Gatecliff Shelter*, by D. H. Thomas, pp. 353-390. Anthropological Papers of the American Museum of Natural History, 59.

Todd, Lawrence C. 1987. Taphonomy of the Horner II Bone Bed. In, *The Horner Site: The type site of the Cody cultural complex*, G.C. Frison and L.C. Todd, eds., pp. 107-198.

Orlando, Fla.: Academic Press.

Todd, Lawrence C. and David Rapson. 1988. Long bone fragmentation and interpretation of faunal assemblages: approaches to comparative analysis. *Journal of Archaeological Science*, 15: 307-325.

Usher, Peter. 1971. The Canadian Western Arctic: a century of change. *Anthropologica*, n.s., 13: 169-183.

Wheat, Joe Ben. 1972. The Olsen-Chubbock site, a Paleo-Indian bison kill. *American Antiquity*, 37. *Memoirs of the Society for American Archaeology*, 26.

White, Theodore. 1952. Observations on the butchering technique of some aboriginal peoples. *American Antiquity* 17: 337-338.

Wilson, Michael. 1980. Population dynamics of the Garnsey site bison. In, *Late Prehistoric Bison Procurement in Southeastern New Mexico: the 1978 season at the Garnsey Site (LA-18399)*, by John Speth and William Parry, pp. 88-129. Ann Arbor: University of Michigan Museum of Anthropology. Technical report 12.